Supporting Children's Learning

Supporting Children's Learning

A Guide for Teaching Assistants

Lyn Overall

$SAGE Publications
London • Thousand Oaks • New Delhi

SAGE Publications Ltd
1 Oliver's Yard
55 City Road
London
EC1Y 1SP

SAGE Publications Inc
2455 Teller Road
Thousand Oaks, California 91320

SAGE Publications India Pvt Ltd
B-42, Panchsheel Enclave
Post Box 4109
New Delhi 110 017

British Library Cataloguing in Publication Data
A catalogue record for this book is available from the British Library

ISBN 978-1-4129-1273-0
ISBN 978-1-4129-1274-7 (pbk)

Library of Congress Control Number: 2006932151

Typeset by Dorwyn, Wells, Somerset
Printed in Great Britain by The Alden Press, Oxford
Printed on paper from sustainable resources

Contents

Tasks

Boxes

Figures

Tables

About the Author

 **Lyn Overall** is Principal Lecturer at Sheffield Hallam University. She is an experienced primary school governor and she works regularly with teachers and children on managing learning in the classroom. She enjoys working with Teaching Assistants on SHU's Foundation Degree, with trainee teachers on primary and secondary routes and on the Playwork degree. She is involved in HLTA work both on the local steering committee and as an assessor.

Acknowledgements

It has been a great pleasure to write this book and a challenge too. I would like to thank many colleagues for their suggestions and wisdom about what to include. To the psychologists, special thanks for your patience in answering, then answering again, the many questions I have asked. Any errors or omissions in this book are entirely my own, not theirs.

I want to thank the many teachers and teaching assistants and workers in non-school settings who have let me into their worlds; it has been a great pleasure to see them in action, to play and work with the children and young adults that they support, and to listen to their ideas on what works and what doesn't.

Finally, thanks to the editorial and other staff at Sage, especially Jeanette Graham, for their help.

Lyn Overall

How to use this book

What is this book about and who is it for?

Teaching is a complex activity; moment by moment there are decisions to be made in helping those we work with to learn. It would be useful, but very boring, if there were recipes that we could apply, if every time we set out to teach we just had to work through a set of instructions. We may think we are teaching a topic with well defined learning objectives, 'to know ...; to be able to ...'. But children and young people may be in another place, more concerned about what is going on in their own heads than what you are trying to teach. We are not working with robots, we are working with people. What is in our heads is not necessarily in theirs. What they learn may not be what we intended. This means that even when we think the teaching has gone well, at the same time we nearly always have issues about its successes and failures.

Bearing in mind that the book has been written for teaching teams, I hope that others will also find it interesting. Schools and early years settings are an important part of children's and young people's lives, but most learning goes on beyond these places. For me, parents and carers are heroes. Playworkers also undertake sterling work in helping children to learn.

This book is a broad brush attempt to introduce the discipline of psychology as it relates to supporting learning. The psychology introduced here will help to inform the choices we make about what to do in our teaching and to underpin the actions that we take. To do this, though, we need to reflect on our teaching and then put these reflections into practice. To be effective the teaching cycle has to be systematic. In other books, I have suggested, with a colleague, the steps that are involved in the cycle:

1. Identify the cause for your concern – name the issue.
2. Consider the available strategies.

3. Select a strategy.

4. Try it out.

5. Did it work?

6. If yes – keep it in the repertoire.

7. If no – select another strategy and try again (Overall and Sangster, 2003a: 8, 2003b: 8).

Naming the issue, deciding what needs to be addressed, starts by looking for the positives in our teaching, identifying what went well about a session, 'the learners were on task most of the time' – and thinking about the strategies that helped with this: eye contact, verbal praise, careful preparation, the particular things you did on that occasion. At the same time you will have noticed issues that you want to address: a particular student's misbehaviour, some information that was not quite understood by learners, the session ending was not smooth, whatever your careful thinking leads you to want further to consider. There may be many issues you could select for attention. But to try to deal with too many would not be profitable so part of the reflective process is to be selective, to deal systematically with the two or three issues you will choose to address in the next sessions. There will be a range of strategies that you can choose from, either those you have thought about for yourself, or you have seen, discussed with colleagues, or read about. Steps 3 and 4 put your plans into action. Steps 5, 6 and 7 evaluate the success, or otherwise, of your teaching in implementing these strategies. This brief explanation of the cycle of teaching is more than likely what you already do. The psychology described in this book will help you to think about the choices that you make. It should enable you to understand and be able to explain why you select and use one strategy rather than another.

It is our curiosity about how learning happens and how to support this that is behind this book. My students' questions, 'why do they do that?' and 'how do they do that?', have been the basis for what to include and what to leave out. It is their reflections made using the cycle of teaching that have provided the stories that I tell. I think that it is great to see children and young people flourish, and I know that some of that success is down to those who work with them: parents and carers, playworkers and teaching teams. My view about teaching is that, if you enjoy it, then it is the best job in the world. It is seldom boring, often frustrating, and sometimes joyous. My hope is that this book will answer some of the questions you have about development and learning.

Psychology is a fascinating subject but it is often frustrating because the answers it provides do not directly answer the questions we ask. Like any discipline it has its mysteries, sometimes impenetrable jargon, and methods of working and thinking that seem designed to make outsiders keep their distance. This book is for people who apply psychology to their work, particularly teaching assistants, but also teachers and undergraduates on teaching, education, early childhood and playwork degrees. Teaching assistants working on a daily basis with children and young people are concerned about their progress and aware of the dilemmas in teaching. They are rich in experience and interested in, but often without much previous knowledge about, the discipline of psychology.

Each chapter in this book sets out to ask questions and describe ideas, and ends with a summary of the main points and suggestions for further study. Throughout each chapter there are tasks for you to do and additional information supporting the chapter's themes appears in boxes. The glossary towards the end of the book explains the key terms used.

Study Guide

As you read each chapter you will find tasks that are designed around particular issues. You can successfully complete most tasks on your own, but some are for use in groups.

The further readings from books, sections from books, articles and websites are included at the end of each chapter both because they are accessible and also to take you a little further in the journey of understanding the relationships between action and the underlying theory. Appendix 1 also includes suggestions for further reading and offers you some ideas about what to expect from these books.

Each of the self study sessions outlined below will take between three to four hours to complete.

Suggested self study timetable

Chapter 1	Learning and development	Session 1
Chapter 2	The brain and learning	Session 2
Chapter 3	The senses and learning	Session 3
Chapter 4	BIG theory 1: Skinner	Session 4
Chapter 5	BIG theory 2: Piaget	Session 5
Chapter 6	BIG theory 3: Vygotsky	Session 6
Chapter 7	Managing learning	Session 7
Chapter 8	Managing discipline	Session 8

Session 1: Chapter 1 Learning and development

This chapter sets the scene by exploring theory, the principles of research into human actions and the key issues in learning and development. It asks questions about nativism or empiricism, continuous or discontinuous, stability or change dichotomies.

Task 1.1 Informal theories
This task introduces some feeling for the methods that can be used to research humankind. It also asks you to begin to think about research ethics and some of the main methods used in research. *Follow-up reading*: Keenan (2002), Chapter 3.

Task 1.2 What's inherited and what's not?
This task offers a chance to think about both your genetic heritage and your acquired knowledge. *Follow-up reading*: Keenan (2002), Chapter 4.

Task 1.3 What is development? Evidence from pictures
Finding a sequence of pictures and using these as evidence about growth and development can be supported by reading Keenan (2002), Chapter 2. The second part of the task uses the National Portrait Gallery's website which is an activity that reminds us about the different ideas that there are about childhood. The third part is about what we can learn from media images. *Follow-up reading*: Bee and Boyd (2004), Part 6.

Session 2: Chapter 2 The brain and learning

This chapter provides a brief introduction to some aspects of brain development. You are invited to learn more about the brain's anatomy and to think about the ways in which things like colour, light and sound levels work to support learning. The policies about early learning arise, at least in part, from the work of brain scientists. A general question is, are some settings more conducive for learning than others? 'Hothousing', that is, providing extra stimulating settings and activities for babies and toddlers, is one of the issues. The colour of the walls, the visual impact and the noise level for settings beyond the home could be issues to be addressed by teaching teams.

Task 2.1 Finding out about the brain
The interactive models from the BBC website enables you to explore the anatomy of the brain. Enjoy the quiz, you will find the most possible answers

are in Appendix 2. *Follow-up reading*: Blakemore and Frith (2005), Chapters 2, 11, and 12; Winston (2003), Chapters 1 and 2; on the Canadian government web pages you will find a very interesting paper (Doherty, 1997) which begins to explore brain development, 'Zero to Six: The Basis for School Readiness – May 1997' on www.sdc.gc.ca/en/cs/sp/sdc/pkrf/publications/1997–002557/page 01.shtml

Task 2.2 School is a foreign country
This task invites you to think about where you work. Do light levels, noise levels and other aspects of the setting impinge upon learning?

Session 3: Chapter 3 The senses and learning

This chapter describes how sight and hearing work. Kinaesthesia is introduced. You are invited to think about how the senses may determine a preference to learn in particular ways. The way the senses work together is illustrated by considering some of the complexities that the learner meets in learning.

Task 3.1 Checking sight and hearing
Think about your results of checks in class on sight and hearing. What can be done to include the learners with sight and hearing that is less than adequate for school learning? *Follow-up reading*: Blakemore and Frith (2005), Chapter 5.

Sessions 4, 5 and 6: BIG theory

This introduction to theories about learning and development spans three chapters. Chapter 4 is about behaviourism with an emphasis on operant conditioning as proposed by Skinner. In teaching we use this theory a great deal, we reward successes. Generally this can be thought of as the control approach to learning. In the next two chapters the guidance approaches to learning are introduced. These approaches put the learner in the centre of the picture, seeing teaching teams as the experts who support and guide. Chapter 5 is about the impact of Piaget and cognitive development theories on our teaching. Chapter 6 introduces Vygotsky and social cognitive theory. The summary for all three chapters is provided in Table 6.2.

Session 4: Chapter 4 BIG theories: An introduction; BIG theory 1: Skinner and the behaviourists

Task 4.1 The shaping game

This task provides an introduction to operant conditioning. A group activity and also a great party game, it is a useful way of beginning to think about how theory underpins what we do in classrooms. *Follow-up reading*: Keenan (2002) provides more general information about behaviourism.

Session 5: Chapter 5
BIG theory 2: Piaget and the constructivists

Task 5.1 Piaget's conservation problems

This task offers opportunities to discuss how research is conducted, but to do it you will need to 'borrow' some younger learners. *Follow-up reading*: Bee and Boyd (2004), Chapters 6, 7 and 8; Donaldson (1978) Introduction; Coleman and Hendry (1999), Chapter 3; Smith, Cowie and Blades (2003), Chapters 12, 13 and 15.

Session 6: Chapter 6
BIG theory 3: Vygotsky and social constructivism

Task 6.1 Design a teaching task using Vygotsky's ideas

Use this task as a starting place for thinking further about how we plan for learning. Analyse your solutions by thinking about the match with the summary provided in Table 6.2. *Follow-up reading*: Keenan (2002), Chapter 6.

Task 6.2 What would you have done?

These stories raise some issues about teaching and are preparation for the final chapters. There are no right or wrong answers. Some teaching requires that decisions are made instantly; sometimes we get this right, sometimes not. You may like to identify when you are using the control approach and when the guidance approach to teaching. And you may like to think about the consequences of the approaches that you choose on the learners. When we make the right decision we need to note it for further use; when we do not, we need to do something about it. The cycle of teaching mentioned above can help to make reflection a routine part of practical teaching.

Session 7: Chapter 7 Managing learning

Applying theory to managing learning means that there are many issues to consider. This chapter starts to explore some of them. As you read think about the consequences of using either the control or guidance approach to learning. When do you choose to use one approach rather than the other? Why is that?

Task 7.1 'I know that now'
This task offers the chance to reflect on 'ah ha' moments in our own lives and relate this experience to learning theories. *Follow-up reading*: Fox (2005), Chapters 6 and 8.

Session 8: Chapter 8 Managing discipline

Discipline, the management of good order in school, is considered in this chapter. As you read, think about the consequences of using either the control or guidance approach to issues about conduct. When do you choose to use one approach rather than the other; why is that? Using the reflective cycle of teaching set out on pages xiii and xiv may help you in the tasks.

Review Task 6.2 and Task 7.2.

Task 8.1 What is misbehaviour?
When learners' conduct becomes inappropriate is the point you may wish to consider. I often sing, hum and whistle but I would not do any of those things in the company of other people. One way of thinking about misbehaviour is as an opportunity to raise learner sensitivity about what is acceptable and what is not. The option of doing nothing can be under-used in school. Sometimes it is best to let learners sort things out between themselves.

Task 8.2 Managing an event
Our aim is to help learners to develop self-regulation and self-control. The task offers the opportunity to think carefully about the choices that we make in discipline. If you can, you should discuss what you think with others.

Follow-up to both these tasks: Revisit your school's policies on discipline and anti-bullying, thinking about how the principles they set out fit with the ideas in Chapter 8.

CHAPTER 1

Learning and development

This chapter begins to answer these questions:

- What is theory? What can we know and use?
- What are the issues in learning and development? Nativism or Empiricism? Continuous or discontinuous? Stability or change?

In thinking about some answers we will meet cavemen, a Greek philosopher, the birth of psychology, and today's theories. We begin to consider the impact of psychology and other knowledge on teaching and learning.

Theory, what's that?

What do you think of these statements?

- 'I always take an umbrella with me, it stops it raining.'
- 'You wait ages for the bus; then, three come at once.'
- 'Children born on a Sunday always have a sunny nature.'

These are the sorts of informal theories that many of us have about day-to-day events. In the first statement the umbrella is like a lucky charm. If I take one with me, perhaps it won't rain; however, it is actually quite unlikely that having the umbrella with me stops the rain from falling. Likewise it is unlikely that the length of the wait and the number of buses that arrive have anything to do with each other. And, whilst some Sunday-born children have a sunny nature, not all of them have.

We all hold informal theories about how children learn and how they develop. Sometimes our intuitive, common sense theories are absolutely correct; what feels right exactly matches a particular moment. Tom is struggling to read 'winning'. To keep your attention he sounds out '/w//i//n/' and says 'win'. At this point you are wondering whether to help, but something holds you back. He gazes hard into your face and says, with a finger on the word, 'is that bit *ing*'? You nod, he smiles and says 'win … ing', 'it's winning'. It is common sense to give beginner readers of any age some space to work things out for themselves. In this case it is good theory too.

Task 1.1 Informal theories

My own deeply held theory is that I will always find a parking place exactly where I want one to be. Over time I have convinced my passengers about this theory. They too are convinced that if they come with me there will be a convenient parking place. But, is it true? I decided that I had better find out. For 150 consecutive journeys I kept a tally. On 64 out of 150 journeys I was able to park exactly where I wanted to. Is that good enough proof? As less than half the journeys resulted in a convenient parking place, clearly my theory is, in fact, not reliable or valid.

Think about one of your informal theories. One, that many of us hold, is that you only have to sit down to eat for the phone to ring. What would you do to test your theory? Perhaps you'd keep a count of the number of times this happened. How long would you keep your experiment going? What level of proof would you accept as good enough to accept or reject the theory?

Now think of a theory that you use with children and young people. Perhaps when you are giving instructions you always say them twice. Perhaps you always wait for 30 seconds before repeating the instruction. You do this because it seems to work for you. But does it? Again, think of ways you might test your theory. What level of proof would you accept as good enough to keep it in your repertoire of strategies?

Often our actions based on common sense are correct and we can use them without causing harm. Sometimes, though, our observations mislead us into making an error by choosing to act in a way that is not going to help. You hear the noise of books and kit being tipped all over the floor, and without looking you call out, 'Sam, what have you done?' Sam is, after all, the usual culprit. Nine times out of ten it would have been her fooling about. But, on this occasion, it was not Sam; it was another student and it was a genuine accident. Sam now has reason to resent what you did and you have to spend time rebuilding a relationship with her.

When working with learners we need theories that will provide a good reason for choosing one course of action over another. When choosing one teaching strategy over another the research that supports it should help to inform our choices. We are looking for theories that are robust, that are more often right than wrong. The theories and research that we choose to use in our teaching will not fit every learner or every context but, often, they will provide a powerful explanation.

We want theories to be reliable. Suppose you wanted a settee to fit into a particular space and the only thing you could find to measure with was a length of elastic. You might stretch it just the same in the shop and at home. If you do this the settee would fit perfectly. But that is quite unlikely; as a tape measure, a piece of elastic is pretty unreliable. The formal theories used to explore how children and young people learn and develop have to be reliable for them to be useful, they have to work more often than not.

As well as being reliable, theories have to be true. The three statements that begin this section are not always true, and those that we thought about in Task 1.1 are only sometimes true. To be useful, theories have to be valid. Using a piece of elastic to measure is not likely to give us a true measurement; we want measurements that we trust. That is why we use a tape measure which gives, providing we take care, a true reading every time. On the whole, we know that the relationship between carrying an umbrella and the likelihood of it raining is down to chance. The explanation about bus frequency is unlikely to have anything to do with the length of time we wait; usually it has much to do with traffic or staff or breakdown problems.

It is worth noting that as we are dealing with human beings, theories will only be valid and reliable up to a point. Sometimes a trusted teaching strategy goes wrong and does not work. The class which does not settle, which ignores our normal signals for 'pay attention', means that we need to revisit our repertoire and find a different strategy for managing this aspect of discipline.

If theories are to be useful then the way that they are tested is important to us. We want to know that consideration has been given to being fair both in the way that the test is conducted and to the people taking part, that the ethics used are acceptable. To test whether children born on a Sunday have sunny natures we might have chosen to ask the parents and carers of all the children born in Sheffield on a particular Sunday. Suppose that most of the parents and carers agreed, 'my Sunday-born child has a sunny nature'. We might conclude that being born on a Sunday does result in having a sunny nature. But the way the result is arrived at has all sorts of flaws. We are not told how many children are involved. We do not know when, how or what was asked about the children. We might get a different result if we choose to ask about Sheffield children born on a different Sunday. We have no idea whether the Sunday-born Sheffield children are similar to Sunday-born children in our own area. Whilst it seems to be ethically acceptable and it probably involved little or no risk to the people taking part, we would not trust a result gathered in this way. We would rightly conclude that the result was not valid or reliable, and we would not take any actions based on such a dubious result.

Learning theories and development theories are tested and built in different ways. One way might be that a single question becomes the focus of research. The researcher becomes very interested in a particular aspect of learning or development. From observation he or she thinks that there is a question that could provide an answer that is worth having. He or she will think about ways to investigate the question, investing time in deciding which of many approaches to research seems most appropriate for the task. The research study will be run, the data collected and then analysed in some way. In working on the answer to the original question, other ideas will then seem to be important and these lead to more research. This cycle of question, test for an answer, leading to another question, then another answer, can often be a lifetime's work. The theory that results will be based on many pieces of research each of which adds to the explanation.

Sometimes this will lead to great big theories that try to give a complete explanation for something that happens in a child's life. This is painstaking work and not all research is on this monumental scale. Sometimes we are offered a single piece of research that hints at an explanation for a tiny aspect of a child's development or the way in which learning happens. At other times the theory is based on thinking about and putting together evidence from many sources, using the work of many researchers, once again offering an explanation that seems to fit. What the best theorists do is to try to think about aspects of learning and development systematically; to provide an analysis that is robust. When this is successful it provides us with help in understanding the children and young people who we work with.

Theory and practice

When thinking about how the results of research apply to our work there are four points to make. The first point is that the context of the research is always something to consider, this includes understanding the underlying beliefs about the world that investigators have. The context and the values we hold colour what we do with children and young people. When working with whole classes we tend to be quite formal; when working one to one we may be much more relaxed. Investigations try to be objective and research is set up to search for truthful answers. Researchers and theorists are people with beliefs and values and they work in contexts which influence how they think about the world. It is worth remembering this when we try to evaluate the usefulness of results. If the researcher's views are a long way from our own, then that research finding may be less effective for our work. Ideas about the usefulness or otherwise of a particular approach to teaching will colour our use of particular strategies. In teaching reading, there are strong opinions about the ways that readers learn the sound symbol relationships, and how much phonics are needed to crack the alphabetic principles of English. Similarly there are different ideas about aspects of teaching maths and science and other school subjects.

Point two is simple: what is regarded as good theory today may be not so sound tomorrow. Knowledge is not fixed, as new evidence and new ways of investigating learning and development become available, theories once thought to offer a perfectly good explanation fall out of use. Up until the late twentieth century the rule was 'spare the rod and spoil the child'. Now even giving a child an occasional smack as a punishment is not thought to be good practice, and in school settings in many countries it is not a legal punishment so must not be used.

The third point is that very often the researcher's work does not match our needs. Not all research is immediately useful to those of us who work or live with babies, children and adolescents. The researchers have their questions, we have ours; our interests and those of the researcher are different, often very different.

What we need to do is to use the 'by-products' of the primary research to help us out in our work. We can use spin-offs from the research that do seem to answer our needs.

The final point is that there will always be exceptions to the theories we use. We all tend to think in dichotomies – up/down, rich/poor, happy/sad – and this is also a feature of academic disciplines. It is a way of thinking about issues and finding questions that may lead to conclusions that can apply widely: seven-year-olds can throw and catch, teenagers argue, happy parents have happy children. The problem is that whilst many seven-year-olds can throw and catch, some cannot. We try, in teaching and related work, to recognise each individual as unique. We use knowledge about groups to make judgements about what someone ought to be able to do, and we compare what the individual can do with what we know the others can do. But if we are wise, we do not expect everyone to learn in the same way or at the same pace; we use what we know about each learner to make plans to assist learning for that particular person. Most respond well to praise, this motivates them to work hard and behave in ways that suit classroom settings. But there will always be one or two individuals in the class who do not respond to praise; they may need a different teaching strategy.

Even the best theory is only a guide to our actions. These are good reasons for keeping up to date, making sure that the theories we use to support the actions we take are current.

The big themes

Where did it all start? Our curiosity about ourselves is ancient. We cannot be sure that this was debated in the flickering light of the stone age fire, but it seems likely that it was. Perhaps, like us they asked this question:

• Is what you are born with fixed or does everything you experience make a difference?

I like to think of Mum and Grandma talking about the youngest boy. They look at him fondly as they sit in the firelight, something in his way of sitting having caught their attention. 'He's just like his dad,' one says to the other. 'Yes, isn't he', says the other. Fantasy, of course, but there is something about these themes that recurs for each generation. Certainly, the debate about what we are born with and what we learn has been there from the start in the written record. Perhaps the oldest and most central theoretical concern for thinkers, this dichotomy is referred to as nativism versus empiricism.

Task 1.2 What's inherited and what's not?

My little finger is smaller than average. My father's little finger is smaller than average, so was his father's. Clearly this is a genetic characteristic. In some families the children don't look much like either parent. Usually though, there is something which lets onlookers spot a family resemblance.

Think about your own family. Is there something which is distinctive, that seems to be a genetic characteristic? Sometimes it's things like having ear lobes that are similar; often it is the shape of the nose, or the whole head.

It is easy to accept that there will be some sort of physical resemblance that can be accounted for by genetics. What about other characteristics? Are these inherited or do they come from the environment? When her daughter was a toddler, a colleague used to say that she 'could argue for England', adding, 'she doesn't get that from me, it's got to be from her father'. The daughter, now an adult, still is very determined.

What do you think? What are we born with? What do we learn?

In the cave did their debate include the other big question?

- Is learning and development messy: does it stop and start, or is it smooth, with one thing following neatly after another?

This is referred to as the continuous or discontinuous question. Wrapped up in this argument are ideas about stages in learning and development.

Added to this are questions about stability and change.

- Does everyone change over time, or are we fixed at some stage and unchanging?

Values and beliefs

The ideas we will meet in this book have to be understood against the central questions of the times. Ideas about human nature continue to influence the questions that psychologists ask. In the seventeenth century these were about sin and redemption: philosophers asked the question, 'is man essentially good or irredeemably evil?' In some religious codes, like Christianity, babies are born as sinners and have to be baptised to be reborn to gain the help of the Holy Spirit to live the good life. In some philosophies, one of which is humanism, people, including children, are seen as good and as seekers of experiences that make them grow and flourish. Even today these questions seem to be important in understanding the theories that we meet.

This is true for teaching teams too. The values and beliefs that we hold have a great influence on our teaching. Teaching teams are usually invited to contribute to the philosophy statements that schools make. If these are a true reflection of their views then the several thousand that I have read are optimistic about human potential. They suggest that most people can learn, and this is reflected in the teaching strategies chosen, the amount of time and effort that is spent with learners who 'don't get it' and the positive attitude that is held about school. Often it is only when it is very hard going that negativity slips into the thinking and comments are made in the privacy of the staffroom, 'thank goodness class x is about to leave, they're a nightmare to work with!' Even then, when challenged, the person making such a remark will usually find something positive to say about the individuals in the class.

Nativism versus empiricism?

In the ancient world the philosopher and teacher Plato believed that some knowledge was inborn. Because of his fame and influence this idea, at least in western thinking, tended to be uncontroversial right through to the seventeenth century. At this point the debate seems to have been revived. The central theme that the French philosopher Descartes and the English philosopher Locke used in this debate is about human nature. Descartes (1596–1650) took the Christian view, whilst Locke (1632–1704) is much nearer to humanist ideas. Descartes' ideas about knowledge, like Plato's, follow the nativist argument. John Locke, by contrast, challenged Descartes' argument; he assumed that, at birth, the mind is like a blank piece of paper, a *tabula rasa*, and that everything that the baby becomes is shaped by experience.

Early in the nineteenth century, ideas about learning and development were worked out by many of the pioneer researchers. These researchers were the inventors of the new science of psychology. One of them, G. Stanley Hall, used Darwin's theory of evolution to inform his views about child development. He thought that there is an inborn development plan, enabling us to identify the average age or norm at which the aspects of development occur. His observations lead to expectations that by a certain age babies would hold their heads up unsupported, then they would crawl then stand and so on. Clearly this is the nativist side of the debate.

Empiricists took a different view. John Watson was one of them and he invented a new term, behaviourism, for his theory. He defined this as developmental changes that occur because of the environment. Watson saw psychology as a totally objective science. He looked at animals and people in exactly the same way, carefully observing what happened when learning took place (Watson, 1913). He even claimed that he could train a child to become good at any job, 'regardless of his talents, abilities, vocations and race' (Watson, 1930: 104). He suggested this would be done by carefully designing the experiences the child would meet, making sure that success was rewarded; simple building blocks to build complex behaviour patterns.

These two researchers, Stanley Hall and Watson, represent opposing views. Although at the time their thinking was entirely modern, the latest thing, these days neither view would be supported. Today ideas and research focus on what we are born with and how this is worked on by our experience; how our nature, or heredity is changed by all the things that happen to us. The dichotomies are still used but the question to be addressed is not: 'is it nature or nurture?', but 'how, exactly, does one act on the other?' Research that addresses the nativism/empiricism dichotomy often asks questions about the interaction of heredity with experience.

Box 1.1 Finding ways to study development: nativism versus empiricism

Is it what we are born with or the things that happen to us and that we do that make us who we are?

Because psychology is the study of humankind, psychologists have to be ingenious in the methods they use. Sometimes you will read a research study where the methods used seem cruel. In the 'Little Albert' study, John Watson deliberately set out and succeeded in making a small child frightened of furry animals and men with beards. These days this kind of study would be ➤

considered unacceptable but in its day, the early twentieth century, the research was acceptable. The outcome of the study, the theory of classical conditioning, was thought to be worth the distress caused to Albert. For Watson, it was one study in a series that helped to confirm his view that the context of learning is all important. Because of his belief in empiricism he was able to suggest that any child could be trained to become what the trainer wanted (Watson and Raynor, 1920).

Albert Gesell, working at almost the same time, adopted a quite different approach and came to a different conclusion about human development. Gesell pioneered the use of film in observational studies. He had a complete commitment to naturalistic observations. Drawing his conclusions from many hours studying children's growth, he thought that many aspects of development were the result of time; babies crawling before walking is an example of what he termed 'age evolution'. His was a nativist explanation, and his approach to research seems much more benign (Gesell et al., 1949: 44).

Nowadays we would think of both these theories as being too simplistic to explain the links between what we are born with and the influence of the environments in which we grow up. Amongst the most interesting research into this relationship are studies of twins. If we think about it, the perfect people for a research study into questions about 'is it nature or nurture?' are identical twins. Identical twins share the same genetic patterns because they develop from the same fertilised egg. In effect they are the same person, and if they are raised apart then developmental psychologists have a splendid opportunity to measure aspects of development. These studies, as you can imagine, are quite difficult to arrange as the researchers have to find sets of twins who for some reason are brought up separately. There are a few though, such as two American studies which show that what intelligence quotient (IQ) tests measure is mainly genetic (Scarr et al., 1993; Loehlin et al., 1994). Both studies used IQ tests on each twin and the mothers. One child in each pair had been adopted and brought up separately from the other twin. These are two more pieces of evidence that may show that the context in which children develop has an effect, but what you are born with is also important.

It should be added that there is another whole debate about what IQ tests actually measure. Generally, they are paper and pencil (or these days, screen and mouse) tests that measure aspects of one child's performance against other children of the same age. Most tests try to capture candidates' ability to reason abstractly. This is only one aspect of intelligence; others include the ability to learn from experience and to learn from the environment or setting.

Continuous or discontinuous?

Do we change gradually over time or does development stop and start? In the first model growth and learning are thought of as continuous. One thing leads smoothly to the next, learning and development are orderly, neat and tidy. In the other view they are discontinuous. Things stop and start, development seems untidy, jerky, fast at one point, slow at another. In the discontinuous view of development the idea of stage is central. Piaget (1952) was interested in how thinking develops. He suggested that children move from one distinct stage of development to another and that these are age related. Between the ages of 7 and 11 children think concretely, needing to use artefacts to understand. In adolescence thinking becomes more abstract.

Box 1.2 Jean Piaget: the child as problem solver

Jean Piaget, a Swiss biologist, suggested a theory of development that has been and remains highly influential. Piaget (1952) describes the baby who learns to reach for something, perhaps a ball, as having learned to co-ordinate a variety of skills, for example staying in an upright position, moving the arm, seeing where the arm has to go in order to grasp the object. Piaget calls this the grasping the object scheme. A variety of previous acquired skills work together to enable the baby to seize the ball. The new skill, grasping the ball, is integrated with what is already known. What if instead of a ball, baby wants to pick up a slice of apple? The scheme for picking up the ball has to be differentiated. The baby's grasp for the ball has to be refined and changed in subtle ways to create the pick up a slice of apple scheme. This is the child as problem solver, a central idea when thinking about learning and development. We will meet Piaget in Chapter 5 BIG Theory 2: Piaget and the constructivists.

Reflecting the question of continuity and change in learning, Siegler (1998) suggests that these two ideas come from the ways in which development is studied. If we look at the development of the ability to understand something, plotting actual changes carefully over time, it may look continuous. He suggests that this is because the changes may be very gradual. In the classroom where we see the same children and young people everyday, the changes are sometimes imperceptible. It takes a break for us to notice that they are getting bigger and more skilful. Suddenly after the Easter break, there seems to be much less space in the classroom because, without us noticing, they have got bigger. Or we notice that some students who had sought help with tasks no longer need this.

At the same time, if we look at development at a given age, it may look discontinuous. Individuals in the same class can differ widely in what each of them can and cannot do. We expect that as learners get older they will know and be able to do more in the subjects that are taught. This means that when we look for individual development in literacy and numeracy at 7, 11 and then at 14, we expect to see differences.

Perhaps both aspects of development are happening at the same time. Some aspects are smooth whilst others occur in jumps. Certainly many young adults, but not all, seem to grow in spurts. All at once, it seems, clothes that were a good fit the week before are now too small. Some children at 12 seem just that, still children, others at the same age are young men and women. You may have noticed this when children are learning to read as well. One week Shamir is struggling to recall sight words, the next it seems she knows many more. Learners sorted in sets to match their learning needs at the beginning of term have remarkably different achievements after five weeks. If we are interested in particular aspects of learning these are what we will notice and what will influence what we do. It is what we choose to pay attention to that influences what we see. This is why in the moment by moment assessment that goes on in teaching, the more careful our assessment the more likely it is that our teaching will match the needs of learners.

Stability or change?

If you are friendly, are you friendly in the same way throughout your life? Or are you more friendly at some times and less friendly at others? If the answer to the first question is 'yes', then some aspects of development are stable. If the answer is 'no', then some change is clearly part of development. Freud and Erikson, in different theories, suggest that the warmth of the relationship between parents and children has a long lasting effect on some aspects of personality. Early experience, they both suggest, is the key – popularly you will hear a mother saying about a daughter, 'I was just like that'. Even so, just because it is observable and seems to be common sense this does not really make it into a sound theory.

In most classes quiet, middle achieving learners are least memorable. Ask

Task 1.3 What is development? Evidence from pictures

A picture can be worth a thousand words. For this task you need to collect pictures of one person, perhaps you or someone you are close to, taken over the years. Assemble them in date order. Your first sort through may be guess work! See if you can put the baby pictures together. Is there a picture of the person as a toddler? If you've been lucky, there is often a picture for every year the person was at school. Are there pictures with different settings? Are there holiday pictures?

Now look at the sequence carefully. What do you notice? If the person is you, you'll have lots of additional information as well. You'll know what it felt like to be you in at least some of the pictures. If it is someone you know well you can ask him or her about the pictures. What memories are triggered? Use the sequence to think about growth and development. Think about a statement that you can make about physical growth from the picture evidence. Are there other statements you can make? Using our own stories is a useful starting place for thinking further about some of the questions about development.

It is interesting to think about how childhood is understood through the use of pictures. Our own experience of childhood is not the same as those of earlier generations. If you go to the National Portrait Gallery (www.npg.org.uk) you can search through 700 pictures of children by going to and using the 'search the collection' link to children. Here you'll see how previous generations viewed childhood. You will notice that until quite recently children were seen as miniature adults.

A final source for this task is TV images. These give us some ideas about childhood in other cultures. Bart Simpson gives us ideas about childhood in the US. News pictures give us ideas about childhood in a variety of countries, not always in the happiest of circumstances. If you watch out for pictures of childhood you'll begin to see them everywhere.

anyone who teaches whose names they learn first and it will almost always be the individuals who draw attention to themselves. Often it will be the noisiest, the learners with the most difficulties and the cleverest whose names are recalled. This view of these learners can persist throughout their school days. If the learner is thought of as 'noisy', is it because he or she really is? Or is it because we think of him or her as noisy? And if thought of as noisy, does the learner act up to our expectations? Perhaps if we start to think of the learner in a different way then there will be subtle changes in our attitudes and expectations towards them. Or has the learner changed? Or because our idea about the learner has changed do they respond to the slight differences in our way of treating them? These ideas about stability are remarkably complex once we start to think about them.

Box 1.3 Stability and change

Challenges to 'common sense' theory come from sources such as research into the dreadful experiences and disrupted lives of orphaned Romanian children (Rutter et al., 1998). The children studied were re-homed with British families. Many of the children in the study were identified as having many problems. One aspect of the study looked at physical growth. The Romanian children were considerably behind the milestones in growth of a group of British children of the same age. What the study revealed was remarkable and rather unexpected. The re-homed children caught up with the British children with whom they were compared. They became physically similar very quickly. However, it is not yet possible to know what effect the early deprivations of the Romanian children will have long term.

How is theory developed?

The recurring themes that developmental psychologists ask are about empiricism and nativism, continuity and discontinuity, and stability and change. These days they seek to study the interplay between apparently conflicting ideas. They find answers to questions through a variety of methods. A good theory will be both valid and reliable, and the research that arises from this theory will stand up to close scrutiny. It will be the subject of debate, as the exploration and scrutiny of ideas is a central academic discipline. One researcher will challenge another's work. Another researcher will build on the original research to gain even more understanding about what is being studied. This work is made available through academic journals, which can often be read on the internet. Later come definitive books in which the theorists explain the research that supports their ideas. And even later still textbooks are written which introduce a wider audience to some of these ideas. When teaching teams (teachers and teaching assistants) meet the ideas from research they may start to think about what they do with learners, how the research supports or challenges the things we each do with children and young people.

How is theory used?

In school and other settings the ideas, the pictures that spring to mind when we think about growth and development, are influenced by our own experience. You will hear comments like:

- 'He's big for his age.'
- 'He behaves like a much younger child.'
- 'Typical teenager, can't stop being loud.'

How accurate are these remarks? If we think about it, some may be, indeed are, suspect. We might want to question whether all teenagers are loud all the time. Nevertheless, we do go on making judgements in our daily dealings with children and young people. This is part of our role, we have to make these assessments in order to make decisions about how to teach. When we seek to make careful objective observations and then try to match these against the development milestones, we are being empirical. Then we can make normative statements, 'he is big for his age', because there is evidence to support the comment. We know that young children may scream to get attention but, as they get older, we would expect that this behaviour will be replaced by requests for help.

We have expectations about appropriate behaviour and learning. These expectations are related to both how old the learner is, their gender and how bright he or she appears to be. We have ideas about how to group learners, by gender, by age, by ability. As well as this, our underpinning theoretical knowledge about what can be done in school subjects supports us in the daily round of teaching and learning. The teaching cycle uses information based on research about learners and our reflections about what they can do and should be able to do to inform the choice of learning strategy.

Summary

Theories are important to each one of us. They influence what parents do with their children, regimes in hospitals, what to do with orphans, how to let play happen and how to teach children in schools, nurseries and the clubs and societies we run. This may not have been the theorists' intention. It may be one of the spin-offs from a theory that has given ideas about how children should be reared. Nor is this process of moving from theory to action straightforward. Knowledge that comes from theory changes over time, what was accepted practice at one time would now be thought of as barbaric. What we do today may not be what we will do in a few years time, as it too may then seem outdated and strange. Empiricism and nativism, continuity and discontinuity, stability and change are central themes in the study of psychology. These are examined and re-examined by theorists and researchers in the search for a better understanding about development and learning. We use this information in implementing the cycle of teaching.

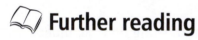 Further reading

The themes addressed in this chapter are central ideas in developmental psychology. This means that all the textbooks have chapters about these themes. Here are four examples.

Bee, H. and Boyd, D. (2004) *The Developing Child* (10th edition). Boston: Allyn and Bacon/Pearson.
This is a standard textbook for students in America on teacher training courses. It is accessible and useful. (A new (11th) edition of this book is due in 2007).

Coleman, J.C. and Hendry, L.B. (1999) *The Nature of Adolescence* (3rd edn.). London: Routledge.
An excellent textbook for anyone interested in teenagers.

Keenan, T. (2002) *An Introduction to Child Development.* London: Sage.
A textbook for psychology students. Chapters 1 and 3 expand on the material presented in this chapter.

Hewstone, M., Finchman, F.D. and Foster, J. (eds) (2005) *Psychology*. Oxford: Blackwell.
This is the introductory textbook prepared for the British Psychological Society for students studying psychology at university. Chapters 1 and 2 provide a comprehensive introduction to the science of psychology and its methodologies.

CHAPTER 2

The brain and learning

This chapter focuses on the brain and some aspects of early learning. You've heard the phrase, 'you're amazing', and so you are. What is truly amazing about each one of us is our brain. Think of the brain as the most sophisticated control system capable of doing all sorts of complex things at once. Its activity keeps us breathing, blinking, sensing movement, hearing, it enables us to move and, above all, to learn. This chapter looks at:

- What is the brain?
- What does it do?
- Learning and the brain

What is the brain?

Obviously, it is what is inside our heads. Enfolded in layers of membrane and fluid, the brain is soft, grey tissue. It is rather like a jelly in consistency so it needs the protection of the bones that make up the skull. The surface is covered with folds and wrinkles. The adult brain weighs about three pounds (1400 grams). Inside this boring exterior is something extraordinary. There are a huge number of cells, around 100 billion. Some of these are neurons. There are also glia cells (which are glue like) which are very important in protecting the brain by gobbling up any dead or damaged material. They also form myelin, which provide the neurons with a layer of fat, rather like the plastic on the outside of electric cable.

Looked at under a microscope, neurons are beautiful. Each one is made up of

Task 2.1 Finding out about the brain

By far the easiest way to become familiar with the anatomy of the brain is to use the excellent interactive facilities of www.bbc.co.uk, following the links to science and nature > human body and mind > brain > brainmap. You can search by function – find out where the 'sad' brain is or which bit enables you to see – or by structure.

When you have explored the brain's anatomy you will be able to answer these questions. The answers are in Appendix 2.

1. Which is the largest part of the brain?
2. What connects the two halves of the brain?
3. Name one of the functions of the frontal lobes which develops at about eighteen months.
4. The motor context controls movement. Which other part of the brain has a co-ordinating function in movement?
5. Which part of the brain is known as the mammalian brain?
6. Which bit of the brain controls breathing?
7. Why is Wernicke's area important?
8. Where is speech production controlled?
9. What are the hippocampus and the frontal cortex responsible for?
10. Which bits of the brain are responsible for self control?
11. Name two things that the amygdale does?

dendrites and axon. The branches at one end of the axon are called dendrites (a Greek word relating to a tree). Inside the neuron are the chemical messengers, neurotransmitters, that let information pass from one cell to another. The bump at the end of the axon is where the neurotransmitters leap the synaptic gap between it and the dendrite of the next neuron. The membrane that surrounds the neuron has gaps in it that allow this to happen.

What does the brain do?

The control system analogy is quite useful for some of the functions of the brain. When we eat we do not need to think about swallowing or digestion, we do not often think about breathing, or the circulation of the blood around our bodies,

Box 2.1 Studying the brain

Brain scientists (usually neurologists) have ways of getting inside our heads to explore what is going on. The trick is to use devices to measure the tiny amount of electrical activity that the brain produces. Neurologists' experiments involve using a machine to find out which parts of the brain are active. They might want to find which bits of the brain control the big toe. (This is not such a daft idea as it first appears if we think about Christopher Reeve, the actor, who damaged his spine and would have dearly loved to have been able to wiggle his toes.) They might tickle the toe then use an appropriate machine to work out what happens in the brain. They give volunteers tasks in order to observe changes in areas of the brain. The changes can be increases in electrical activity, in magnetic activity or in blood flow. There are different machines to measure these processes. The Science Museum website has a section on 'watching the brain work' that shows pictures and provides clear explanations: go to www.sciencemuseum.org.uk and follow the links to exhibition > brain. Here is a list of some of the machines that are used to examine the brain.

- **EEG Electroencephalograph** To make this work electrodes are stuck to the surface of the scalp. The toe would be tickled and the brain's electrical activity recorded.
- **MEG Magneto-encephalograph** This machine uses magnets to measure the brain's magnetic field and thus its electrical activity. MRI Magnetic Resonance Scanners and fMRI functional Magnetic Resonance Scanners give deep and surface three-dimensional images of the brain. TMS Trancranial Magnetic Stimulators uses weak pulse electric magnets to stimulate particular areas of the brain.
- **PEP Positron Emission Tomography** When the neurons fire they need oxygen and oxygen is carried by the blood. This machine looks at blood flow in the brain.

All these techniques are non-invasive. This is a considerable improvement to the early research in this area which was often conducted on patients with horrific head injuries from which doctors made deductions about how the brain worked. Even today most research will be medical in origin, with scientists seeking solutions to conditions like Parkinson's and Alzheimer's or how to mend broken backs.

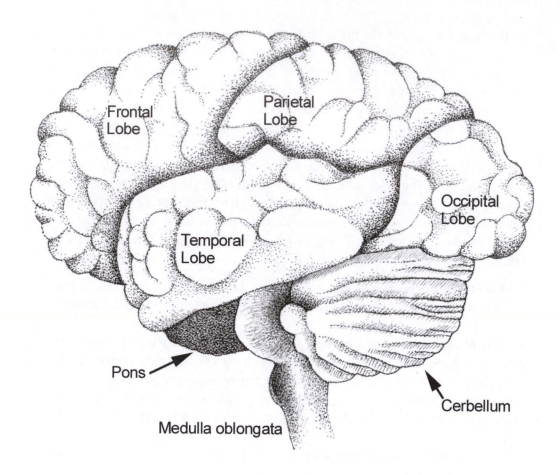

Figure 2.1 The anatomy of the brain, viewed from the side.

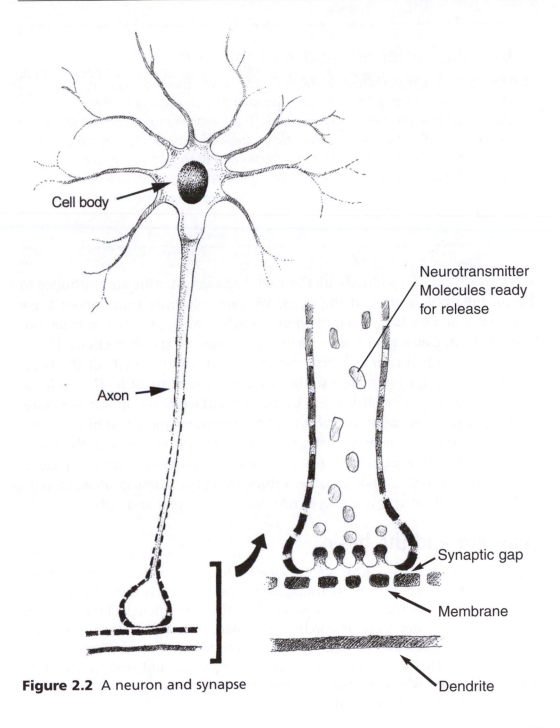

Cell body

Neurotransmitter Molecules ready for release

Axon

Synaptic gap

Membrane

Dendrite

Figure 2.2 A neuron and synapse

Box 2.2 Preferred modes of thinking

There are some myths about the brain which you will have come across. You may even have tried out tests which suggested that you were left or right brained, or that you were 'whole brained'. These tests are fun to do but this is 'pop psych' rather than serious psychology. The idea behind this is that the two halves of the brain have different functions: that the left half of the brain deals with maths, logic, analysis, and the right with the creative, the emotions, the subjective. However, the truth is that to do most things you use both sides of your brain most of the time.

or our hearts pumping blood – all these vital processes for life are controlled in the medulla oblongata and the pons. We probably only think about these functions when we have eaten too much or when we are too hot or when our hearts pound. Getting up from a chair is organised by the cerebellum. This is the part of the brain that governs our movements. Other parts of the brain help us to process information so that we can make sense of it. The occipital lobe helps us to use what we see. Under the surface is the limbic structure, drawing things together so we can learn and remember and know how we feel. It is the connections between each neuron in the specific areas of the brain, and between each area, which makes these things happen: turning a page in this book will involve, amongst other things, using the language areas, co-ordinating fine movements, wanting to read more of the text and sight.

Learning and the brain

The brain changes as we learn and because we learn. At present there are three issues that influence the way we think about this. The first is about the connections in the brain made in the first year of life. These are thought by some to be extremely important. Some researchers are asking, 'Are there ways that these connections can be helped along?' There is a second set of issues about whether there are moments when learning happens more easily and readily. The third question is about whether a rich learning environment is central to changes in the brain, or if learning happens anyway.

Brain connections, birth to one year

One set of ideas suggests that it is the work that parents and carers put in playing with the baby that helps the changes in the developing brain. This is a beguiling thought, but it is not clear whether doing more makes a difference to the brain or not. What happens in the brain, how are connections and pathways made? At birth the brain begins to complete its growth by making the connections, or pathways, between the cells. At first this happens very rapidly. In baby brains the numbers of connections are very many more than in those of adults. In fact there are too many connections so part of the development is for the brain to reduce or prune those which are not needed. When we place our fingers in the newly born baby's hand the grip is instinctive; you put your finger there and the baby has to grasp it. But by three months baby is making choices about whether to be interested in your finger or not; he or she will more than likely find a waving finger interesting to look at and will make a conscious choice to reach out to grip it. What has happened between birth and three months is that the brain has changed.

At around three months the visual cortex has started to make the connections at the front of the brain; these new connections begin the process that will replace the instinctive grasp of the new born. Between four and five months babies are beginning to know which toy is being offered as they begin to see edges, colour and movement. By around a year the baby will happily play 'peek a boo', using his or her memory and sight to make choices about where to look for the toy which we first show then hide. The brain has in some way reorganised itself, though we are not sure how this happens.

Does the brain learn some things more easily at some points?

On the whole, no matter where they are done studies of brain development show that the development of visual, movement and memory functions happens at about the same age. If you are an English or a Russian or a Chinese baby your brain at the same age will let you do similar things. Brain development in the early stages does not seem to be about race, or gender, or the way in which you are brought up. Despite this, the second issue is about whether there are magic moments, what brain scientists call critical or sensitive periods, when learning some things are easier.

Wiesal and Hubel, who won the Nobel prize for their work in the 1960s, found that if at a critical period a healthy eye in young animals is covered, this results in that eye not being able to see (Blakemore and Firth, 2005). For the brain to learn how to see the eye needs to have light and activity at a time when the connections in the brain can be made. It used to be thought that if these critical periods for the development of connections for sight were missed the eye would never work. But the brain can catch up if, fairly soon after being covered, the eye is uncovered and then gets the stimulation it needs at this point. The brain connections that allow sight can then be made.

Robert Winston (2003), writing about the development of the visual cortex, reminds us that the early excitement about this idea when applied to children who were born without sight was most disappointing. Indeed, the results were horrific and upsetting. These children, when given new lenses at around age ten, were unable to adapt to the light that flooded into their eyes. It seems that their brains had lost the ability to change, the plasticity that enables the necessary connections for seeing to be made. Even when the experiments with animals were apparently successful, what is unclear is whether the quality of the sight is the same as if the brain had made the connections at the earlier point. Nevertheless, rather than the implication of a particular and specific point which once past is gone for good, it seems likely that there are several periods when the brain is sensitive to making the connections for seeing. Beyond a certain point though, it was thought that the brain will not be able to make the necessary pathways or connections. The same seems to be true for the development of hearing and other senses. But more recent work is much more hopeful. With the right input it seems it may be possible to create new paths, new connections, in the brain that will enable sight and, by implication, hearing (Winston, 2003).

Parents and carers are rightly concerned to identify any sensory losses early, and where possible put this right. Often what is good enough for home surroundings becomes a barrier to learning in school. This is why it is important that teaching teams help by regularly carrying out informal checks on the sight and hearing of children and young people, to make sure that they can benefit from the teaching offered. Chapter 3 has more about how this can be done.

Does brain development need a rich and varied setting?

You hear of parents who give their babies nurseries which burst with colour, that are filled with music and have every kind of toy, where baby whilst awake has an adult who continuously talks and plays with him or her. This is often called 'hothousing'. The intention is for these babies to develop their brains better and faster. The Romanian orphans, on the other hand (see Box 1.3 Stability and change: p 14), came from settings that were stark in the extreme. Certainly, this study shows that such neglected babies had delayed development in many areas. Yet when placed with carers who offered a normal home life most of these orphaned babies made remarkable recoveries. Their development caught up with other children who had a normal start. There is really no strong evidence either way for hot-housing being either helpful or harmful; the studies have yet to be done. On the other hand, using the Romanian orphans research, we can draw the conclusion that without parents or carers to react to, without a safe place, adequate food and care, the baby's brain and other aspects of development may be harmed.

When children get to school and throughout their school years we should consider what makes some classrooms better places for learning than others. This seems to be an area of practice where such information that is available is not widely used. Where teaching teams 'own' the space, think of it as their teaching

Task 2.2 School is a foreign country

In this chapter we are thinking about what the brain may need to use the experiences it meets. Let's see if this helps us to think about our own workplace from the point of view of the people we teach. No matter how much preparation we do with the children and young people who come to our schools, they are still very different and distinctive places. For learners joining the play at nursery or playgroup, and at the transitions from preschool to first class, from infants to junior, junior to secondary and onwards, the situations that they meet are unique. At home, however large your family, it is familiar territory; my premise is that all schools are at first, strange new worlds.

Most schools have programmes to bridge the gaps between home and school, school and a new school, year group to next year group; the people and ways of working are often carefully and thoughtfully introduced. A year 6 child having spent a day at her secondary school came home bursting to tell everyone all about it: 'They were nice to me ... lunch was great ... and in the afternoon we did proper science with Bunsen burners'. We seem to think ➤

about this aspect of progression. But what about the bits that we seem not to think about?

This task invites you to view your workplace as though for the first time, to consider the look of the place and the noise levels. Attempt to put yourself in the child's/young person's position by working out what their experience might be. How would you rate:

The classrooms?

Visually calm	About right	Visually busy
Noisy	About right	Quiet
Too light	About right	Too dark

Other indoor spaces?

Visually calm	About right	Visually busy
Noisy	About right	Quiet
Too light	About right	Too dark

Outdoor spaces?

Visually calm	About right	Visually busy
Noisy	About right	Quiet

Using the same scale, where would you place yourself?

Visually calm	About right	Visually busy
Noisy	About right	Quiet

Choose a colleague, where would you place him or her?

Visually calm	About right	Visually busy
Noisy	About right	Quiet

What impact do you think your school's visual appearance and noise level has on those you work with? Are there some who do not thrive because it is too noisy, too visually busy? What about the light level in the teaching space you work in most often? Could the lighting from either a natural or artificial source be better?

If it was in your power, what changes would you make?

Box 2.3 Can the brain's ability to learn be improved?

There are a great many ideas which suggest that the answer to this question may be 'yes'. This is not the same as 'hothousing' which tries to increase the rate of brain development. Certainly, the ideas mentioned here will not do any harm and if they do some good that is a bonus.

1. A dietary supplement of fatty acids came out well in a recent UK trial. Children with learning disorders such as dyspraxia who were given dietary supplements of Omega 3 fatty acids (which are found in fish oil) made significant gains in their test scores, attitude and concentration levels (Reading, 2005). Omega 3 EPA seems to make the sending of messages between the brain cells more effective. Whatever the reason, there is an increasing interest in this idea by researchers. Because of the highly controlled nature of the research this piece of evidence seems convincing. In Durham they have extended the trial to many more children and young people. Another larger scale study is taking place in Middlesbrough with similarly promising results. On the manufacturer's Omega 3 products website www.equazen.co further details on these studies and new developments can be found.

2. You may have seen 'Jamie's Dinners' (BBC TV, 2005). This programme became a catalyst for action to improve children's health and wellbeing, and, we hope, their ability to learn by making school food more nutritious. As, for many children, school dinner is their main meal of the day, this seems to be a commonsense move. The body, including the brain, does better if it has the right foods. As well as protein and fats, complex carbohydrates are thought to be important.

3. It is now policy in many schools to allow children access to drinking water. The thinking behind this is that the brain does better if the body is not thirsty. Many children seem not to recognise that they are thirsty. They, especially younger children, need to be taught to recognise when they are thirsty and encouraged to drink. It goes without saying that sweet fizzy drinks (have you seen the lurid green one?) are not satisfactory substitutes for plain drinking water (www.waterforhealth.org.uk; Kleiner, 1999; Rodgers et al., 2001). ➤

4. Giving the brain a mental workout, something that gives the short-term memory exercise, like mental maths, seems promising (Kligberg et al., 2005). For many years Tony Buzan (2003) has been doing this with ideas like mind maps. On the basis of use it or lose it, ideas like brain gym also have a following (http://www.braingym.org.uk).

5. The Mozart effect, where Frances Rauscher (1994) and his co-workers discovered that rats ran mazes faster after listening to classical music, continues to be of interest. It is suggested that music lessons give a boost to pre-schoolers' scores on spatial reasoning tests (Holden, 2003). However, McKelvie and Low (2002) come to a different conclusion, suggesting that the improvement was not to do with music lessons but more to do with the context that music lessons evoke. Rauscher (2003), reviewing a number of studies, reminds us that we should not expect too much either from listening to or studying music. On the other hand, perhaps music seems to have a calming effect and enables some children and young people to pay better attention which could be what makes the idea appealing.

6. There are many common sense aids to better brain work as well. When reading something that requires full attention, a simple command to myself of 'pay attention' seems to help. What this does is to raise my attention level: rather Zen perhaps. In the classroom children can respond well to this approach. Try giving them an agreed key word to help refocus attention. Cutting down on distractions is another way of letting the brain get on with it. Bright and cheerful classrooms can be too visually stimulating for some children. Other learners find noise distracting; they would prefer to work in very quiet conditions. As you might expect, the right amount of sleep and the right amount of exercise are also thought to be important in getting the brain to work well.

room, thought needs to be given as to what sort of stimulation will help the learning. The research pages of the University of Georgia on learning environments (www.coe.uga.edu/sdpl/researchabstracts/visual.htm) suggests that colour preferences seem to be varied: some learners favoured neutral walls and floors whilst others like bright colours (http://www.coe.uga.ed/sdpl – follow the link to research > abstracts 'Colors influence on attitude'). Good lighting seems to feature quite highly in the research. The noise level is also something that most teaching teams consider. I suppose that most teachers and teaching assistants find that the introduction of carpeted floors in school helps make it less noisy and that this helps learning. Certainly most school discipline codes have noise reduction as an item. At the same time classroom displays are thought to be an important aspect of the learning provision. Whilst the evidence about colour, lighting and display seems to be flimsy, we can observe 'custom and practice' in our own workplaces and think about how this impacts on learning.

We know that the brain is amazing. We know something about how it works. But in reality we still know very little about how most human brains develop from birth to about ten years. By contrast we do know a great deal about cognitive development from birth to ten. We know a great deal about how children become able to talk, to listen, to be social beings, to learn to read and write. We also know about how their mathematical and scientific knowledge develops. What we do not know, directly, is what is going on in the brain when these things happen. We know that even a few days after birth babies can tell the difference between two and three objects. As there has not been enough time for this to come from the home, the conclusion has been made that some sort of maths ability is developed in the brain during the time in the womb (Dehaene, 1998). We know that the brain changes but not exactly how this happens.

Increasingly we can expect to understand more about what changes occur in the brain as we learn. What is starting to happen is that in studying development cognitive psychologists are working with brain scientists. They are bringing together their different disciplines to use knowledge about cognitive development to search for and provide explanations about what happens in the brain. Ingenious bits of kit are already able to map some of the things that happen in the brain when we look at a picture, hear music, react to pleasant or unpleasant smells. Most of these measurements require the person seeing the picture or hearing the music to be static. It is likely that very soon the changes that happen in the brain when we do more complex learning will be able to be measured in more natural settings, such as classrooms.

Summary

In this chapter the emphasis has been on early development in the brain and the possible relationships with learning. We know with some certainty that in order to thrive babies need to have contact with adults in settings that lets their brains develop; if these conditions are denied then babies do not reach expected developmental milestones. Whether hothousing gives an advantage is not known, as there is not enough evidence as yet to make a judgement. Giving Romanian orphaned babies a more normal setting shows that the brain does seem to have the ability to play 'catch up'. Whether the development is the same as it would have been had it happened at the expected time is not clear. In our own settings we can think about the impact on learning of light levels, colours and noise levels. Whilst the impact on learning may be slight, taking every advantage to help the brain seems sensible. Finally, cognitive neuroscience is finding even more ways to study the developing brain. The results of these studies are likely to be very useful for anyone who is interested in learning.

Further reading

There are an increasing number of books about cognitive neuroscience which are for a non-specialist audience. My choices are below and they will extend the introductory knowledge included in this chapter.

Blakemore, S-J. and Frith, U. (2005) *The Learning Brain: Lessons for Education.* Oxford: Blackwell.
One writer is a neuroscientist and the other a cognitive psychologist: both are interested in autism and Uta Frith is also involved in dyslexia research. They have put together a textbook that introduces some of the complex ideas in brain science and learning. Chapters 2, 11, and 12 are recommended as supplementary reading for this chapter.

Winston, R. (2003) *The Human Mind and How to Make the Most of It.* London: Bantam Press.
Robert Winston presented an excellent BBC series *The Human Mind*, and the resulting book is a really interesting read. Try Chapters 1 and 2 as supplementary reading for this chapter.

On the Canadian government's web pages you will find a very interesting paper 'Zero to Six: The Basis for School Readiness' (Doherty, 1997), available on www.sdc.gc.ca/en/cs/sp/sdc/pkrf/publications/1997–002557/page01.shtml which begins to link information on brain development with schooling. Think about the research that is used to make the argument presented. Do you accept the argument that the paper makes?

CHAPTER 3

The senses and learning

This chapter explores aspects of learning both to see and to hear, and considers kinaesthesia and learning. Whilst all the senses have a role to play in learning, think of the ways certain smells bring memories flooding back, or the way it feels to touch smooth velvet, or the pleasure of the perfect move in a favourite ball game. It is just that we seem to use our sight and hearing and kinaesthetics much more than the other senses. The questions explored in this chapter are:

- What is perception?
- What is involved in seeing and hearing?
- How are the senses used in learning? An introduction to VAK – which stands for **v**isual learning, **a**uditory learning and **k**inaesthetic learning – a teaching approach that uses learner preferences.

Sensation and perception

The other day, out shopping for a new outfit, a friend said to me, 'I like that colour green'. My response surprised her, 'It's blue to me'. As far as I know there is nothing particularly wrong with either of our sight, and I think we both know our colours. It seems that she categorises the colour turquoise as a green whilst I have it in my range of blues. So what is going on here? Our senses gained the same, or to be strictly accurate, very similar information from the light that came from the material. The light entered through our respective eyes, hit the colour receptors at the back of the eye, the information rushed to the visual cortex in our brains: mine says 'turquoise = blue', hers says 'turquoise = green'. Our senses received the same information but our brains understood it differently. We might see in similar ways but our perception, our interpretation, is different. We have come to a different meaning for the same input.

As the conversation continued, 'turquoise', we agreed, was the colour we were both seeing; we have both achieved colour constancy, the ability to see colour as remaining the same even when in different lights. The phrases, 'can't you see?', and 'I see' that are so common suggest that we are not talking about the 'something' itself but the message that this 'something' involves. These phrases, indeed conversation in general, are a way of checking shared perceptions. Our ability to see and hear things in similar ways is taken for granted in most teaching settings. We expect those we teach to perceive the world as we do. This is why we are surprised when those we work with miss out an item on a worksheet that we thought obvious. When we give an instruction such as 'sit, thanks', we may have a picture in out minds about what this means: typically bottom on a seat, feet on the floor. We only have to glance round any class to see that 'sit' means something very different to many in the room.

Studying perception

The perceptual abilities of babies have been much studied. Once babies were thought of as having little or no sight at birth; now we know that they see much more than we thought. You cannot ask very young children 'what can you see?', but it is possible to set up experiments were the researcher can observe where and what the baby looks at. One early approach was to simply show the baby two pictures and time how long the baby looked at either picture. Another approach is to get the baby used to something, to the point where a new sight or sound is not interesting, then to introduce another sight or sound, and to see what happens at that point. The third approach is where baby learns to turn towards a sight or sound and the experimenter then uses the learning in a systematic way to explore baby perception.

Perception studies are a useful example of the nativist versus empiricist argument. The nativist view has some strong support. After all, babies do not have to be taught to look. They can recognise their mothers by sight, smell and sound from the earliest moments. The empiricist argument has some points to make as well. If babies do not have the opportunities to look then their ability to do so is much less than those with normal opportunities. Recognising particular faces it is pretty clear is built in, but the number of faces the baby is able to recognise depends on the opportunities he or she has to look at different faces (Slater et al., 2000). It looks as though there is both an inborn and experience base to becoming able to recognise faces. So the argument is not is it inborn or learned but rather what is the relationship between what is hard-wired (the nativist view) and what is acquired later, empirically, through experience.

Seeing

Babies are born able to see clearly close up things: the breast or the bottle will be in focus but someone by the door will be out of focus. By about 12 months they have normal vision, and from this point on their visual acuity, the quality of the vision, including the ability to make finer distinctions, improves until about the age of five. Object tracking improves rapidly too. Even new born babies can track a toy when it is moved from side to side. Aslin (1987) suggests that at this stage the newborn is seeing the edges but over the next few weeks the eyes begin to look all over the toy. And whilst colour vision may be present from birth, the ability to use it only develops at around two months. This may be accounted for by the developments in the brain around that time. No doubt this will become clearer as the ability to link changes in behaviour to the areas in the brain which show electrical activity becomes possible. By three or four months babies' sight is very well organised.

The ability to use the information that we see is important throughout our lives. Watching Crufts (a world class UK event in the dog world) it becomes clear that the judge's perceptions have been refined through long experience. Each judge seems to know exactly what makes a top dog and the expert commentators are able to explain why the dog won. Similarly, in football the offside rule takes some experience to begin to see and then understand, and even then the armchair ref. may disagree with the referee on the field. It is not that we learn to see better, but that our experience means that we are more able to interpret and understand what we see. In some ways, perhaps, our perception becomes more refined.

Clearly the way we use what we see is important in many aspects of learning. Some people seem to be able to visualise words easily and effortlessly, their spelling is nearly always correct and they can spot their own errors. As we become skilled at spelling our ability to visualise helps us to check whether all the letters in the word are there in the correct order. Often people who think of themselves as poor spellers have not fully developed this ability. This may relate to ideas about learning styles; generally people seem to divide into either those who visualise or use their auditory abilities, or those who learn through movement, kinaesthetically. When teaching spelling it may very helpful to offer more support to those whose preferred learning mode is not visual. Luke, at 15, almost gave up writing stories and poems because his English teacher kept returning his work because of the spelling errors he made. A family friend found out about this and was able to work with Luke on a variety of strategies for checking his work and for improving his spelling, 'He told me that I wasn't an idiot, just not very good at checking my work. Teachers and my mates always like my stuff but I'd often get comments about poor spelling; Mr X was always saying, "Great story Luke, shame about the spelling." I'd started to think of myself as someone who could not spell. Terry changed all that. He made me pay attention to the order of the letters in the words that I wanted to use. Mind you, it was hard work and still is. And sometimes I use an alternative word rather than go to the bother of looking up my first choice.' Later in this conversation he talked about writing on the computer and the joys and perils of the spell checker. His favourite mistake was using 'manor' for 'manner', which, he said, got a big laugh from his history teacher. Luke's restricted range of learning styles and his understanding about his own learning were the focus of Terry's interventions. Through their discussions he was helped to find ways of coping and improving spelling, and, at the same time, seems to have become much more aware about learning in general.

Box 3.1 Learning to look

What makes these letters tricky for beginning writers?

p   b   d

What makes these numbers tricky?

9   6

Why do some children write 'S' instead of '5'?

Why does 's' get confused with 'z'?

Think about children's early experiences. A cup is still a cup even if it gets tipped over, a chair is still a chair even when it is being used as a cave by being set sideways on the floor, your sister is still your sister even when she is standing on her head. Young children live in a form constant world *until* we ask them to read and write. Then, which way up and which direction letters take becomes important. We have to learn that a 'b' is a different letter from a 'p' and that the reverse 'b' is different again, it is in fact a 'd'. We also learn that '**b**' and '*ƀ*'   ➤

---

and '*b*' and '*b*' and '*b*' – in fact any way the letter is presented – is still a 'b'. Likewise we learn not to confuse '6' with '9', or '5' with 's', or to write 's' as 'z'.

This is about perception. Seeing letter shapes means that we have to discriminate differences. As shape constancy has been measured in babies as young as two months (Bower, 1966), when we then ask children learning to read and write letters and numbers to make very fine discriminations we are asking them to break new ground. Presumably, the brain has to set up some new connections to achieve this. The question is, can we help this process along?

Most children go through a stage when they make these sorts of errors: getting mixed up, not being sure which letter is which, writing '9' as '6', 's' as 'z'. What if learning to discriminate is like the overgeneralisations that children make in speech, when they invent words such as 'wented'? We know that even when corrected to 'you *went*, didn't you', the child will still reply, 'Yes, I did wented'. Yet, very shortly afterwards this aspect of speech will have gone, the overgeneralisations will have disappeared.

If we try too hard to teach the discrimination task it might not make the learning any easier for the child. All the ingenious ways of trying to help them make the distinction may not in fact help. A more laid back approach of noticing when the child gets the letters correct and praising this may be the way to go. Coupled with systematic handwriting teaching, this may be the most sensible way of dealing with this aspect of learning. If we take time and trouble to teach the way to form letters and make this a fun activity – using large movements in the air, in the sand, with big pens on big paper, before moving on to copying exercises – this may help children to move though to this stage. We are drawing their attention to a correct form and giving the kinaesthetic movements to help fix it in the mind.

Some children seem to stick for some time with this; if the learner goes on having difficulty in making letter discriminations then we do need to take action. Assessment will be a key activity. In the moment by moment teaching round, noting when we notice discrimination errors would be the first step. This information needs to be collected systematically and discussed by the teaching team to decide on appropriate strategies. If the errors are persistent then the learner will need an appropriate teaching programme and probably some further investigation. The Special Needs Coordinator (SENCO) will be involved as they have access to more assessment and teaching materials.

Hearing

Have you ever wondered why when we talk to babies we often use a higher pitched voice? We know that babies' auditory acuity is actually better than their visual acuity. They hear nearly as well as adults. We also know that they are less sensitive to lower pitched sounds. It is interesting that rather than treating all sounds as having equal importance, there seems to be a biological preparedness for speech and music. Babies and toddlers react more readily to the human voice than to other sounds. You have seen perhaps a baby turn his or her head sharply to find the person who said something or laughed or sneezed. It is almost as if the question, 'where is that sound?', is said out loud. This ability to track is so well developed that they are even able to find objects, like a rattle, in the dark from the sounds they hear it make.

In classrooms we expect learners to pay attention to what we say. This is both at a general level of instruction – 'do three questions, then check your answers' – and in specific learning such as phonics, where the ability to match the letter with a sound is one aspect of learning to read. Being able to hear the differences in letter sounds helps us to work out words. Luke, whose spelling got him into difficulties, is an excellent listener. He reported that when he was in junior school he would annoy his teacher, who thought he was not paying attention, by giving a verbatim answer using the teacher's exact words when challenged.

Task 3.1 Checking sight and hearing

If you work with children and young people, can you answer these questions?

- How many should wear glasses for close work, like reading or using the computer?
- How many should wear glasses for looking at the white board or big books, any task where they need to be able to focus on a distant object?
- Who needs to be reminded to wear their glasses?
- Who needs to be reminded to clean their glasses?

If you had the names on a list in front of you, could you then answer the questions? Finally, can you answer this question: which children and young people have difficulty in hearing? ➤

While babies and young children have their sight and hearing checked at regular intervals, it is often when they come to school that very slight differences from normal sight and hearing mean that some children and young people make less progress that might be expected.

If you could answer any of the questions you did well. If you wear glasses or have any problems with hearing yourself, you will know how important it is to be aware and alert to the needs of children and young people to see clearly and hear well.

If you are in a position to do some checking on sight and hearing you might find the following checklists helpful. Any suspicions should be tactfully handled with parents and carers who will need to seek appropriate professional services.

Checklist for sight

If you tick five or more on the list, then that learner might have a vision problem. Compare the individual with what you expect from others who do well in the same class. He or she:

1. Reads at a lower level than others in the class.
2. Avoids reading, or other up close tasks.
3. Omits, reverses or confuses words when reading.
4. Loses the place or needs to use a finger when reading along a line of text.
5. Becomes distracted and finds it difficult to remain on task (reading, writing, maths).
6. Has a short attention span.
7. Does better if allowed to take breaks when reading or writing or doing calculations.
8. Tires quickly when reading or writing.
9. Suffers from eye strain.
10. Has red or watery eyes when reading.
11. Complains of blurred, double or moving print.
12. Tilts the head at an angle when reading (to let the preferred eye do the work).

➤

13. Holds the book very close to the eyes or very far away.
14. Covers an eye when reading.
15. Has difficult in paper and pencil tests.
16. Has difficulty copying from the board.
17. Has difficulty working on a computer screen.
18. Reverses letters and numbers after age 8.
19. Never finishes any written work.
20. Appears unmotivated (lazy) when required to do reading or writing tasks.
21. Appears frustrated with reading and writing tasks.
22. Complains of headaches.
23. Has handwriting in which letters are poorly formed, spacing is erratic, writing is not always on the line.
24. Has hand/eye co-ordination that appears to be poor.
25. Can appear awkward or clumsy.

Checklist for hearing

Some hearing loss is normal with a bad cold. A blocked nose usually means that high frequency sounds are lost. Children who have frequent bad colds, or glue ear, are likely to be at a disadvantage with tasks that need sound discrimination such as using phonics. They should have medical help to enable them to hear. To help make a decision, compare the learner with what you expect from others in the same class who are doing well.

1. With younger children speech is not progressing. With older learners the voice is monotonous.
2. Speech is delayed or there is inappropriate speech recognition.
3. The student does not startle at unexpected loud sounds (try dropping a metal tray behind him or her).
4. The student is perplexed when asked to imitate a sound.
5. When asked a question, the student does not turn towards you and may appear to be disobedient. (For example, when you say, 'Clear up, now.' The student whose back you addressed does not.)
6. The student does not hear what is said in the hall, playground or dining room.

➤

7. The student daydreams, seems not to take part in conversation with others.
8. The student has frequent ear infections.

These websites have a wealth of information:
www.ontariosciencecenter.ca >scizone>games>Eyes have it. Or do they?
www.bbc.co.uk >health>healthy ears and eyes
www.bbc.co.uk >science and nature>human mind and body>nervous system>hearing and sight>fun centre>interactive eye
www.bbc.co.uk >science and nature>human mind and body>nervous system>hearing and sight>fun centre>interactive ear

Kinaesthesia

Watching skilled footballers suggests that kinaesthesia is important in learning. They seem to know exactly where the ball is in relation to any part of their bodies without having to think about it. They use their bodies to move, to change direction, jump, swerve, reverse, keeping the ball under control until the right moment arises to make the next move in the game. The kinaesthetic sense can be easily demonstrated. Even with your eyes closed you will be able to write your name. It is easier to tie a shoe lace than explain how to tie one. Your neural memory is sufficient for these tasks, the movements you make are automatic. The practice that footballers have put in, coupled with natural ability, have made ball control something that they can do without conscious thought.

The kinaesthetic sense has become one that teachers and teaching assistants pay attention to also. It is thought to be important in learning. In order to spot the kinaesthetic learner we may need to revise our ideas about the fidgets in the class. The learner who has to doodle and the young child who cannot sit still during the story may well be kinaesthetic learners. Using kinaesthetic techniques to help fix letter shapes, learners may be asked to write them in sand and to feel the movement as they make the letter with an exaggerated whole arm movement.

Making sense

Some people see particular words as a particular colour; for some the word 'egg' (on the page or said aloud) is seen as purple. This linking can apply to the way music may be heard as well; some hear music as colours. Synaesthesia, linking senses in this particularly strong fashion, seems to be the way that we all begin, as new babies, to make memories. Newly born babies use all their senses to make sense of their world. The newly born not only see their mothers, they taste them, smell them and touch them; all the senses are used to memorise who is mother. Babies often explore new objects by looking at them and touching them, often putting them into their mouths. They have the ability to use more than one sensory input to make sense of the object. They find it easy to use their senses to do intermodal perception. Think about baby learning to use a spoon to feed: making the judgement about where the plate is in relation to the hand and grasping the spoon means using sight, movement and touch all together. The process of learning to speak is helped if baby can begin to match the sounds of speech to the movement of the speaker's lips.

Visual learning, Auditory learning, Kinaesthetic learning

When it comes to more deliberate learning, becoming literate and numerate using the senses, using intermodal perception, is going to be vital. Luke described one technique he now uses to fix new words: 'First I double check that I've got the word down right, after all it would be stupid to learn it wrong. Then I say each letter as I write the word. I do this three or four times, carefully checking that I'm getting the word right. When I think I know it, I turn the piece of paper over and see if I can get the word right without checking. If I can, wow. If not it's more practice.' *Look, cover, write (and check)* is a commonly used technique when teaching spelling. It exploits our senses, encouraging careful looking, hearing the letters in the word and, as we write, fixing the word in our neural memory. Numeracy teaching encourages children to use more than one sense as well. A group of nursery children are working with a teaching assistant learning to count. As they chant 'one, two, three, four …', he shows them a card with the number on it. Later they build number tower bricks, excitedly showing them to him and saying the number they have made. Later still, he shows them a number card asking them to say the number. They are seeing, saying and using touch to help fix the number in their memories.

Box 3.2 Dealing with sight and hearing difficulties

Children and young people with sight and hearing problems face similar challenges to those with normal sight and vision in their learning. They will need to make the best use of all their senses to gain the perceptions needed to make the best use of their time in school.

These questions may help you to find appropriate solutions in the classroom for children and young people with *sight problems*. They will improve the classroom for children with good sight as well.

1. What level of lighting is necessary for the student's visual condition?
2. What size of print is best?
3. Does the child need to be close to the board, positioned to one side, or with his/her back to the window?
4. Can the level of visual acuity be improved with glasses or by the use of specialised low vision aids?
5. Are there any restrictions to the visual field?
6. Does he/she have vision in both eyes, or only one?
7. Does he/she display any eye dominance or preference?

For further information use the website at www.nbcs.org.uk
This site for parents and carers of blind children is an excellent source of support for those who work in educational settings.

These questions may help you to find appropriate solutions in the classroom for children and young people with *hearing problems*.

1. Where is the best spot for the learner? He or she needs to see the face of the speaker and the speaker's face needs to be in a good light.
2. Which ear hears best?
3. What aids does the learner use and what aids do you, and other workers, need to make best use of for his/her hearing?
4. What can you expect him or her to hear? What is it unlikely that he or she will hear?

For general information on children with hearing loss consult: Conrad (1979), *The Deaf School Child*. The website at www.ndcs.org.uk is very useful.

➤

This site for parents and carers of deaf children is an excellent source of support for those who work in educational settings.

A useful summary of Sterne and Goswami's (2000) study of the effects of deafness on learning to read can be accessed on www.literacytrust.org.uk following the links to publications where Abram Sterne's article for *Literacy Today* has been archived.

The senses used together, seeing and hearing and movement, seems to be important in learning. There are thought to be three main learning preferences. Many of us are visual learners; we make sense of our world through what we see. For us, our preferred learning style is likely to involve looking. Auditory learners prefer to listen. Others learn best through activity, through the sensations involved in movement; these are kinaesthetic learners. Curriculum and activities for learning are thought to work best if learners' preferences are used in teaching. VAK (visual learning, auditory learning, kinaesthetic learning) teaching develops:

- visual learning through text plus illustration, graphs, maps, visualisation to improve memory, access to CD-Roms, posters, keywords, video, demonstration, memory mapping (e.g. flow charts, story boards);
- auditory learning through opportunities to talk about the work, lectures (i.e. something to listen to), a speech CD, spelling that recalls the pattern through sounds;
- learning through movement, using kinaesthesia, through opportunities to be active, role plays, field trips, design and make tasks, hand and gestures when talking, *look cover write check* for teaching spelling.

VAK has its critics. Riding (2002) is one of these. Rather than VAK he suggests that two cognitive styles should inform teaching. His work suggests that you are either someone who sees things as wholes and in parts; or you talk yourself through tasks and use your mind's eye to learn. Whichever way an individual learns, it is useful when planning learning tasks to provide for the learner's preferences. But this is only half the story. If he had been allowed to use only his preferred approach to learning, Luke might have gone on thinking of himself as someone who does not do spelling. Applying Riding's model to design a treasure map, the children were encouraged to draw first the outline of an island, then to put in the landscape features and so on, until they had completed the task; that is, letting them use wholes and parts. At the same time, task-centred talk was a feature of the whole process from design to evaluation. The teaching assistant who used this task was tapping into both cognitive styles and encouraging flexibility in learning. Using more than one approach means that the learner benefits from increased flexibility. Learners may start by having one learning preference, but may end by being comfortable with teaching that uses other approaches. It may be helpful to think about these ideas in terms of both what we are born with and the strategies that we learn to learn.

Summary

The senses clearly play a very important part in our development. We have explored some of the nativist versus empiricist ideas about this. The light from objects that enters our nervous system has to be interpreted by the brain for perception to occur or the message to be understood. These connections are obviously complex. Learning and remembering means our senses need to work together in quite complex ways. Mastering the spelling in English is an example of this. The task for the chapter should help you to spot the learner who needs some help with sight or hearing. The chapter ended by using ideas about visual, auditory and kinaesthetic learning preferences, introducing the practical use that ideas about learning styles have in teaching.

Further reading

Bee, H. and Boyd, D. (2004) *The Developing Child* (10th edn.). Boston: Allyn and Bacon/Pearson.
Chapters 4 and 5 offer useful introductions to the ways that research into the senses and perception are carried out. A new (11th) edition will be available in 2007.

Winston, R. (2003) *The Human Mind and How to Make the Most of It*. London: Bantam Press.
Try Chapters 3 and 4 to supplement your reading for this chapter.

http://en.wikipedia.org
Use the online encyclopaedia for more on kinaesthesia and synaesthesia.

BIG theories: An introduction to theories about learning and development

Development changes learning; learning changes development. As baby's sight develops, baby is able to learn more about the world; as baby learns more about the world, baby's sight changes. What explanations are there for this idea? This chapter introduces what I term BIG theory. The theories we will meet have an impact that you will recognise in your work.

Every day bits of these theories are used on us and we use them with others. In the classroom, a group of children are rewarded for their hard work on their story writing. They go back to their work with renewed vigour. In some supermarkets, when asked, 'where is …?', staff are trained to leave the task they are on to take the customer to the right place. The pay off for the supermarket is that because staff appear to be helpful, the customer is likely to return regularly, thus increasing that supermarket's ability to make profits. At home, you increase your chances of getting your partner to respond promptly to something that you want done by asking at the psychologically right moment. He or she is more likely to undertake the washing-up, when you have cooked a favourite meal. My cousin was so delighted by her grandchildren putting away their toys without being asked that she took them swimming (a favourite treat).

Often what at first seems like simple common sense is in fact the deliberate use of psychology. The theories we use inform what we do and what others do with us. Thinking about the cycle of teaching introduced at the start of the book, our choice of teaching strategies is better informed by understanding the principles that underpin them. We need to understand the ➤

theory behind our choices because as well as some desirable aspects there may be downsides as well.

This and the following two chapters introduce the BIG theories: the first is about behaviourism, the second is about constructivism and the third is about social constructivism. As far as possible, each chapter follows the same format. Each will introduce the theory or theories, and then begin to explore the principles as they apply to teaching. There are tasks for you to do and books for further reading are suggested. At the end of Chapter 6 you will find a summary for all three chapters, summarising the application of these theories to the classroom.

CHAPTER 4

BIG theory 1: Skinner and the behaviourists

In the nativist–empiricist divide behaviourists are empiricists to a man: for them it is not what you are born with but what you learn that matters. This chapter offers a very brief background to behaviourism, suggesting ways which we use this theory in our work. It looks at:

- Studying behaviour: Animal studies
- Learning through imitation: Bandura
- Implications for teaching: Behaviourism

What is behaviourism?

Central to this theory is a psychology of learning in which the definition of learning is limited because it accepts only what can be observed rather than implied. There is no room for the subjective in this theory. You see a man go into a newsagent. That is your observation. From your observation you might guess that he is going to buy a paper. Skinner, who we will come to shortly, would not allow you to guess: he would have said the purpose for going into the newsagent cannot be known by you. You cannot know for certain, unless and until you make a new observation of behaviour, if when the man comes out of the shop you see the newspaper in his hand. In behaviourism the observation of the behaviour is the object of study: it is about what we do, our actions, not about how we feel about things. I think that behaviourism is firmly in favour of the empiricist side of the nativist–empiricist debate.

The behaviourists

The classical behaviourists are generally recognised to be Ivan Pavlov (1849–1936), John Watson (1878–1958) and Edward Thorndike (1874–1949). Today Burrhus F. Skinner (1904–1990) who extended the work of the classical behaviourists, continues to be influential. Each researcher offered explanations about learning and development in relation to his particular theory. Each one influenced the work of the others and there is a relationship between their respective research. At the same time, each theory is distinct and recognisably different.

The classical behaviourists (Pavlov, Watson and Thorndike) were men of their times and their ideas and ways of working reflect how people thought about things at that time. They were, no doubt, excited by the new ideas that were about: Darwin's theory on the origin of species and Freud's ideas about the unconscious. The nativist/empiricist divide would have formed part of their thinking and their thinking was at the empiricist end of the argument. The world in which they lived moved from the stagecoach to the train, and from the farm to the factory; it became mechanised and industrialised. Their solutions can seem to make people more like machines than perhaps we would find acceptable. Some of the things they did to explore their ideas seem shocking or cruel to us today, whereas for them they were perfectly acceptable. They used animals such as cats, rats, dogs and pigeons in their experiments, arguing that animal behaviours are similar to human behaviours. At this distance, it easy to be very critical about some of their experiments. But here is something to think about: if they had not carried out their experiments, would we know what we do now?

Cat in a box

Pavlov had observed that dogs salivated when they saw the kennel man coming with their food. After some time thinking about this event, he had one of those moments which separate out clever folk from really clever folk. He connected the dogs' salivating with the arrival of food as learning. He is probably responsible for the idea of *stimulus–response*; the stimulus was the arrival of the kennel man with his clanking bucket of meat, the response was the dogs' salivating.

Thorndike discovered that if you placed a cat in a box it would struggle until it found the lever that would release it. Placed in the box over and over again the cat would stop doing those things which were ineffective and eventually hit the freedom lever every time. This happened faster if the hungry cat knew that there was food outside the box, that it could eat when free. This was trial and error learning, but from this and other experiments the *law of effect* was formed. This says that you are more likely to repeat the action that gets rewarded. This is the reason for the small treats that learners get for being 'good', 'for trying hard', 'for getting a correct answer'.

Rat in a box

Watson also used Pavlov's observations. He is credited with the term 'behaviourism'. He studied animal and human behaviour systematically. You will recall from Chapter 1 that in one experiment Albert was taught or conditioned to have the fear reaction (see Box 1.1). Watson and his co-worker Rayner used Albert's startle reflex, a loud noise, to cause him to be frightened by a rat. By the end of a week Albert had generalised his fear to anything furry: a Father Christmas mask, a dog or rabbit (Watson and Rayner, 1920). His investigations started from the premise that there had to be an observable goal, that his animals had to learn something that he had predetermined. His rats were not working by trial and error though. They were introduced to the specific actions needed to complete the task systematically. Once the hungry rat knew that being in the box would mean that it got food, the lever that had to be pressed to release the food was introduced. The primary stimulus, food, is gradually replaced by the secondary stimulus, pressing the lever. Try Task 4.1 on page 52 at this point to begin to understand how the primary stimulus, the chocolate buttons, can be replaced with the secondary stimulus, the click.

Learning through imitation

Most psychologists, indeed anyone who thinks about learning and development, are keen to explore issues beyond those that behaviourists study. One of these researchers is Albert Bandura (b. 1924) whose interests focus on how social behaviour is developed. I suppose we could say that Bandura supports the view that about half of what we become is from our genetics and half from what happens to us as we grow up. His work has refined some aspects of behaviourism. One of his claims is that people learn through imitating the actions of others. This is one of those ideas that appeals because it seems to align

Task 4.1 The shaping game

For this game you need a clicker, some treats (chocolate buttons or similar) and two people: one person to play the 'dog', the other to play the trainer. The audience, whilst optional, makes this game even more fun. This is what you do.

1. Send the dog/person out of the room (out of earshot if your audience is likely to be lively).

2. The audience or trainer selects a specific action for the dog/person to do. This can be anything physically possible but something that won't embarrass the dog/person. Let your imagination run freely for this. To get you started here are some safe, tried and tested ideas: turning the light on, sitting on a specific chair, turning round three times at the front of the room. (I have had a PE specialist turning cartwheels in a precise place but most people can't do that!) Make sure that the trainer and the audience know exactly what they want the dog/person to do. Be precise.

3. The trainer invites the dog/person back into the room.

4. The trainer asks the dog/person to move round the room.

5. The trainer clicks (a clap or 'yes' will do if no clicker is available) to indicate that the dog/person is getting close to the specific action.

6. The dog/person returns to the trainer for a treat each time he/she hears a click. (After the treat the dog/person goes back to the point when the click was given, BUT let the dog/person work that one out.)

7. The trainer continues to click actions that get closer to the specific action until the dog/person does the specific action.

8. Repeat with a new dog/person and new trainer until everyone has experienced both roles.

Remember that the trainer and the audience **cannot** give any verbal cues or signals to the dog/person.

with common sense. Kind children have kind parents – every day the child is encouraged to be kind because the parents are kind to him or her; every day the child is kind the parents are encouraged to be kind back. The link with Skinner's theory of operant conditioning is through reinforcement. But for Bandura the reinforcement is not just from reward or punishment. Bandura suggests it is the information and encouragement we get from the reward that makes the child more likely to be kind. In Skinner's operant conditioning the reward is neutral but for Bandura it is a motivator. Bandura's social learning cognitive theory uses elements from each of the big theories discussed in this and the following two chapters. He tries to make a theory that will fit most learning. You will find out more about his ideas in Box 4.1 (see page 54).

Implications for teaching: behaviourism

Behaviourist ideas are widely used in schools. Many of the teaching strategies used on a regular basis come directly from Skinner's work on operant conditioning. He was most important in developing the science of behaviourism, and his work is widely known and used with both children and adults as well as in animal training. For Skinner, a reinforcement of an identified behaviour will mean that the behaviour will happen again. Thus, if my dog barks and I give him attention, it is likely that the barking will become an established behaviour. This is how it goes: the dog wants my attention so barks, I say 'be quiet', dog barks, I say 'be quiet'; thus the dog has learned bark = attention. The dog has trained me to respond to his bark. Skinner explains this as the *contingencies of reinforcement*. There are some more examples in Table 4.1 below.

Table 4.1 *A B C Contingencies of Reinforcement*

The antecedent stimuli	A behaviour	The reinforcing consequence
Using Skinner's (1969) work Contingencies of Reinforcement *three things can be specified.*		
A Dog barks	B I say, 'be quiet'	C Dog barks for attention
A Student leaves her seat	B I say, 'Jodie, back to your place'	C Jodie knows a sure fire way to get my attention is to leave her seat
A I say, '3+4=?'	B Tim answers '7'	C I say, 'That's right, well done'

Box 4.1 Bandura's social learning or social cognitive theory

Bandura has brought aspects from various theories together to provide a way of understanding and dealing with day to day issues. He started as a behaviourist but now includes a social dimension in his explanations. The main features of the theory are set out below.

Bandura (1977) rejects the behaviourist link between the stimulus and the response as being too simple. You will remember that behaviourists see this link as automatic. Not so Bandura – he suggests that each of us has a choice and that we make that choice quite aware that it will have consequences. Furthermore, the choice will take into account the surrounding events. This may help to explain why one sister is frightened of heights whilst the other is totally happy to sit in the back row of the highest seats in the theatre. They have different reactions to a similar situation. Bandura would suggest that the sisters have learned different behaviours.

Bandura also thinks that what we want and what drives us are important in explaining differences between people. Some children and young people find conforming to school discipline really easy, it aligns completely with the way they would want to act. They know that in order to learn listening to the instruction helps. All the students have this opportunity but not all of them see the need to be obedient; their needs and those of teaching teams are not immediately compatible.

Another aspect to this theory that Bandura makes is that each time we make a choice, the outcome, the consequences of the choice, can make a difference to the next choice. If you are a chatty person and the people you chat to encourage you by chatting back, this can mean that you become more likely to chat. Bandura would suggest that as it works for you, you will chat more often than not. This means that those students who choose not to conform may have their choice reinforced by the actions that teaching teams take.

In the cycle of teaching one way of identifying the issues we wish to address is to use contingencies of reinforcement as an analytical tool. The formulae works like this: A is what provoked the behaviour, B is the response and C is what happened to reinforce it. Having worked out what might be the cause of the issue, then a strategy to address the issue will be easier to select.

Skinner and his colleagues were remarkably successful in training animals. To do this they paid very close attention to ensure that the reward was given at exactly the right moment to reinforce the required response. The other important thing that they did was to identify, very precisely, the response that was to be rewarded. Then they worked out a sequence of actions that would be rewarded to shape the behaviour. This method is used today in training both people and animals, including search and rescue dogs, animal actors, horses and household pets. The cycle of teaching strategies used to address issues will often follow a behaviourist method: the learning objective will be carefully selected, teacher and teaching assistants will work out what has to be done to achieve the objective and implement it by reinforcing appropriately. For us, much of the fun in the shaping game outlined in Task 4.1 comes when the trainer misses the moment and clicks inappropriately. When this happens because the dog/person has been misled it can be very difficult to get back on track. This is what happens in classrooms as well: when we inadvertently reinforce an unwanted bit of learning we have to start over again with the learner to reverse our training error. A virtue of positive reinforcement is that we can avoid punishment and just re-teach.

When playing the shaping game it is possible to see if the dog/person has really learned the specific action just completed, such as *sit on the chair next to the person in the red jumper*. To test whether the specific response has been learnt, the dog/person is asked to leave the room. Whilst out of the room the chair is left empty and in the same position, but the person in the red jumper moves and sits next to another empty chair. When the dog/person returns the person is asked to do what he or she did the last time. You can imagine what happens. The dog/person strides in and confidently sits on the same chair as before: it is rare to get the complete response. Usually the dog/person will get as far as *sit on the chair*, sitting on the vacant chair where the reward was earned the first time. We made the assumption that what the dog/person had learned was *sit on the chair next to the person in the red jumper*. But clearly this is not the case.

What should the trainer do at this point? In operant conditioning the answer is nothing. The dog/person has no reward, no click for *sit on the chair*. The reinforcement is given only when the specific behaviour, the learning objective, is chosen. When the specified behaviour happens every time, then, and only then, has the learning been achieved. In making observations about learning in school the same degree of precision is required. We are looking for a reliable response every time. This is not to imply that Skinner thought of learning as something simple. Far from it. He acknowledged its complexity but he stuck with his ideas, backing them with careful commentary to the end of his life.

You will see in Box 4.2 following that operant conditioning, the relationship between the stimulus and the response, can provide an explanation for at least some of the things that go on in classrooms. Interestingly Skinner thought that punishment was not a good idea. He would always have chosen positive reinforcement as his way of achieving the desired outcome.

Many people use behaviourism in their dealings with others at least some of the time. You may have seen operant conditioning (Skinner's version of the theory) in use in classrooms: children and young people are rewarded for the work they do correctly and they are tested on what they learn. Typically there are practice tasks which offer a reward for success. Teaching teams often use behaviourism as a basis for helping learners to develop self regulation, as a basis for teaching the school discipline code. When teaching classroom rules, teachers and teaching assistants are skilled at rewarding small moves toward rule keeping. They will notice and reward Simon who has kept quiet for two minutes, then set a new target of two and half minutes of not interrupting.

Ideas about being clear about what has to be done seem to me to come directly from behaviourist theory. These days we are all set targets, big or small; we are all asked to action plan; to say what we will do, how we will do it and to say when we will meet the target – this week, next month, next year. It is useful to be clear about what we want to achieve in teaching sessions, what we want the children and young people to know, do, be skilful about, and understand.

The principles in the shaping game can be applied to how material is prepared for use with learners. Having identified the learning outcome as 'treat customers respectfully', the trainers in a supermarket will have broken down exactly what that means into stages. They will have developed training materials in which each step has to be mastered by the staff being trained. In schools, teachers break down complex learning into small steps, rewarding children's and young people's success at each step. Some computer based learning uses a similar process. The downside of this very structured approach is that it may stifle

Box 4.2 Operant conditioning

If you use behaviourism it is worth really understanding operant conditioning. Here are four ways that learning through response to the stimulus can be strengthened.

Teacher praises learner for holding the door open for others to enter a room.

- **Positive reinforcement** REWARD
- Correct response followed by reinforcer
- Strengthens response, learner is likely to continue the behaviour

Teacher stops nagging when the learner reliably holds the door open for others to enter a room.

- **Negative reinforcement** AVOIDANCE
- Correct response followed by withdrawing the adverse stimulus
- Strengthens response, learner is likely to continue the behaviour

Teacher tells the learner off for not holding the door open for others.

- **Punishment** POSITIVE PUNISHMENT
- Undesired behaviours followed by adverse stimulus
- Weakens the undesired response

Teacher punishes the learner for not holding the door open for others by requiring him or her to stay behind in the classroom for part of break.

- **Omission** NEGATIVE PUNISHMENT
- Undesired behaviours followed by withholding of reinforcer
- Weakens the undesired response

spontaneity in learning and creativity. To keep learners engaged the trick is probably about knowing when to abandon the set objective in order to allow for the unexpected, the unusual and the joyous to occur.

Behaviourists are firmly of the view that someone is 'in charge'. Their view would be that if you work or live with children and young people then it had better be you who is 'in charge'. This idea is very appealing. However, I am sure you can already hear the 'but' that is coming. If adults take control all the time where, when and how do children and young people become independent and capable of making decisions for themselves? In our adult lives we are all from time to time behaviourists, but I would suggest that we need other approaches as well. We need a psychology that recognises that in order to be fully human we need more than direction and control.

CHAPTER 5

BIG theory 2: Piaget and the constructivists

'Stage' is such a common part of the vocabulary when we deal with children and young people that it is hard to remember it was once a new idea. We talk about, 'He's at this or that stage', as a sort of shorthand which sets up expectations about conduct, learning and achievement, as well as for development. If we understand that each of us constructs our own understanding then this is another Piagetian idea: he saw learners as doing just this. This chapter explores:

- The work of Piaget
- How well does the theory work?
- Information processing
- Implications for teaching: constructivism

What is constructivism?

The behaviourist will assert that anyone can be taught anything provided the steps in learning are small enough (sometimes infinitesimal) and that they are rewarded appropriately. The learner's interest in acquiring the learning is irrelevant in behaviourism; he or she is the recipient of the training. Constructivism on the other hand places the learner and his or her needs centrally. In constructivism it is the learner whose curiosity leads to the exploration of problems, leading to the discovery of solutions. The important idea is that the learner is active in constructing knowledge. Each learner constructs an understanding about his or her own world. Furthermore, the individual's understanding changes as the learner develops.

The work of Piaget

Jean Piaget (1896–1980) used his own children to begin to develop an influential theory about development. For him the study of psychology had to involve human beings. The study of animal behaviour was not part of his repertoire. Moving from Switzerland to Paris he became familiar with the work of Freud which speculates about why people act as they do. His interest in the question, 'what is intelligence?', was stimulated by his work on the responses to tests designed to understand the nature of intelligence. It seems from the number and range of his published works that he never stopped learning himself. He seems always to have been examining and re-examining his own work, coming to slightly different conclusions. His openness to reviewing his own ideas, to constructing new understandings, is one of the reasons he is regarded as an outstanding theorist.

Piaget's background was that of a trained biologist and he carried out original research in that field. Darwin's theory of evolution is a clear influence on the cognitive development theory he developed. Evolution was for him a central idea, so in human development he was looking for changes that happen over time. Similarly, disciplines such as psychiatry and epistemology – a branch of philosophy that studies knowledge by asking questions such as, 'How do you know what you know?' and 'Do you really know that?' – had a profound influence on his work.

His observational methods can be said to have moved the study of psychology to more realistic settings. He sought understanding in three ways. He observed what children do to solve problems. When the answer the child gave was incorrect he did not assume that the child was wrong, rather he was endlessly curious about their solutions, recognising the differences between adults' ideas and theirs. Secondly he tried things out, conducting small scale experiments to see how the child understood the world. And thirdly he talked with the child. Always he looked for changes in the child, trying to work out the way that he or she began to develop an understanding about phenomena.

Box 5.1 Early studies by Piaget

Piaget used reasoning problems like this to explore children's thinking:

Jim is fairer that Mike. Jim is darker than David.
Who is the darkest, Jim, Mike or David?

The correct answer is *Mike*. But children generally cannot solve such problems until they are about eleven years old. The youngest children will often say, 'David' who is fairest of all.

The explanation that Piaget offers is that children treat darker and fairer as categories (that is, dark and fair) rather than as relational terms. If dark and fair are categories then the following logic works. *Jim is fairer than Mike* means for the children that both Jim and Mike are fair, whilst *Jim is darker than David* means that Jim and Mike are both dark. On this logic David is darkest, he is the only one to be completely dark and Jim is the only one to be completely fair. Mike is both fair and dark. The children's use of categories rather than that of relationships gives them the wrong answer.

Piaget developed the clinical interview as a main method of investigating learning. Seeking to understand a child's knowledge through probing questions, the interview is a particularly challenging way of working because it is so easy to get it wrong and cause the child to clam up rather than letting the questioner into his or her thought processes. His students needed a year to learn this way of working. To explore how children think he presented them with problems and then used probing questions to find out what they understood. He was systematic in his approach, and was soon convinced that the errors that children made can be grouped. His explanations were and are logical and compelling.

Piaget rejects the behaviourist view of the child as responding to rewards and punishments. For him, children are active scientists seeking to understand what they encounter. They do the work to develop their own thinking and understanding; the central idea for Piaget was that each child constructs understanding. They seek to make sense of the events and phenomena that they meet. We were sitting in a café one day when a toddler and her mother came in. Outside the café a big, rather curly coated, white dog was tied up. The toddler, perhaps 19 months old, soon had her nose up against the window and could be heard saying over and over again, 'Not sheep, not dog; not sheep, not dog'. She has, we can suppose, constructed a concept of a dog and of a sheep. She knows what these animals are. The dog outside the window was clearly a new phenomenon. It would be lovely to report that she got to 'sheep dog' whilst we were there, but she did not. She was not able to work that out.

What Piaget suggested was that there are stages of development that relate to the ways in which the child gains understanding. The stages are age related and overlap. Each stage builds on what has gone before. For Piaget the order in which they do this never varies: sensori-motor is followed by pre-operational, then comes concrete operational and finally formal operational. Table 5.1 describes some of the characteristics of these stages. Whilst the order of the stages seems to be consistent for all children, it has been established that the age at which a child moves from one stage to another can vary a great deal.

Table 5.1 *Cognitive development stages*

Stage	Age	Description
Sensori motor	0–18 months or 2 years	Understands: • their world through the senses and by actions, at first randomly then more deliberately • A is not B • object permanence Uses pretend play
Symbolic or pre-concrete operational	18 months–7 or 8 years	Begins to: • represent the world symbolically but intuitively and egocentrically • develop language • dream • play imaginatively
Concrete operational	7 or 8–12 years	Does things in their heads but needs physical props Problem solving Sees the relationships between things
Formal operational	12–15 years	No need for props to do things in their heads Thinks about thoughts Constructs ideals Reasons

The mental process that Piaget uses is the idea of scheme or schema (both terms are used in the translations). Linked to this are two key ideas, accommodation and assimilation. Accommodation is about dealing with input, changing the input to match what is already there – if you like, the bit when we take things in. Assimilation is about dealing with the input by making changes to existing thinking or creating new ways of thinking, being able to understand something new or understand in a new way. The way this works is that as the child encounters a new experience he/she accommodates existing thinking to it and then assimilates aspects of the experience. That point is described as a moment of equilibrium, that balance when something is learned and a new under-standing occurs. In Piaget's theory children, and perhaps all learners, move from one state to another state of mental equilibrium, restructuring thought to create a new state. They construct different understandings from existing think-ing and construct new thinking to make new understandings.

We can speculate that the child in the sheep/dog story is in the sensori motor stage: she is taking in something new but is not able to link this to previous knowledge and understanding to develop a new piece of knowledge. Over time, as they move between the stages, learners become gradually more accurate and have more detailed and complex sets of concepts and understandings about the phenomena, objects, people and events they encounter.

How well does this theory work?

Piaget considered that a child's intellectual development went on all the time, he thought of it as a continuous cycle of developing new schemes through assimilation and accommodation bringing these into equilibrium. One way he sought to demonstrate this was through conservation tasks such as those shown in Task 5.1. In one of these tasks the child, when shown the two beakers with equal amounts of water in them and amazed at the adult's stupid question, will normally tell you just that, 'there is the same amount of water in each'. The water from beaker A is then poured into differently shaped beaker C (either nar-rower and higher, or lower and wider). The child, at Piaget's pre-operational stage, is supposed to say that there is more water in the beaker with the higher water level. When asked to imagine the water poured back into beaker A the child is not supposed to have grasped the principle of reversibility (that actions can be reversed) so will not know that once again the water level will be the same.

Task 5.1 Piaget's conservation problems

You will need access to children up to the age of seven to try out these conservation tasks. Piaget argues that the limitations of thinking at the pre-operational stage are best shown by setting conservation tasks. Conservation means that the child understands that the property of matter is not changed by the ways it is shown.

Property	Stage 1: The child agrees that the two objects are the same with respect to the property	Stage 2: Objects are rearranged and the child is asked whether they are still the same with respect to the property
Volume of liquid in the beaker		

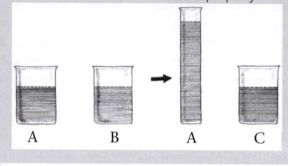

Number of sweets in each row	

Length of each rod

What did you find out? Which children could manage the conservation tasks? What does this make you think about Piaget's theory?

Similar things happen when the row of counters is spread out and when the position of the rod is moved.

One suggestion that Piaget made to explain these conservation tasks is that the child is only focusing on one attribute at a time. The child presented with the longer row of counters may think that there are more counters, not realising that the row is longer because there is more distance between the counters. They are not able to compensate for this difference.

But is Piaget's explanation correct? Is it really true that children at the pre-operational stage are unable to compensate and cannot grasp the principle of reversal? These days the view is taken that Piaget saw what he wanted to see and that when he made a mistake he was somehow unable to accept this. Work by Donaldson (1973) and her co-workers (1983) and, more recently, Siegal (1997) suggests that the children's inability to do the conservation tasks in the way that Piaget set them does not mean that they do not think logically. Donaldson, Grieve and Pratt (1983, Chapter 18) provide many examples of children's ability to think completely logically, and that children of six or seven can reason deduc-tively. Their evidence is completely convincing. They argue that the tasks as orig-inally presented do not make sense to children, that they do not understand what they are being asked to do. In Piaget's experiment counters are used and the emphasis from the experimenter is that the row is going to change. The child uses previous experience to expect that there will be change, that there is going to be a trick. Donaldson's explanation is that this is what misleads the child, that the child is expecting the row to change. The way the task is presented to chil-dren is thought to be unnatural. If presented more realistically using sweets rather than counters, Donaldson reported that many children seem perfectly happy to point out that it is a silly question 'because there are still the same number of sweets' and to explain this by saying 'they are just further apart, so it doesn't matter which row I choose, I'll still get the same number of sweets'. This work has been done time and time again with similar results.

Siegal's (1997) contribution shows that changing the way the questions are asked, even very slightly, can increase the chances of the child's success. He acknowledges that Piaget recognised and tried to put questions in ways that chil-dren could understand. But he points out that Piaget put the child into a test sit-uation. He argues that it is both the situation and the researcher's language that do not allow children to show what they can do as together these were too strange and unfamiliar. What he did to deal with this was to make the tasks more like con-versation, where the researcher and the child seek to discover the answer together.

Box 5.2 What is theory of mind?

Piaget's work on social development has provided a rich area for researchers. Understanding what someone else thinks is thought to be a human characteristic. Theory of mind (TOM) is important because it begins to explain how we fall for advertisements or propaganda, why we lie to save someone from hurt feelings – the white lie – or to protect ourselves when we slightly change a story – deception. However, we are not born with TOM. Children from different races and backgrounds seem to acquire the ability at about the same age. This has lead to the speculation that TOM is a specific adaptation, separate from general purpose intelligence. One of the tests that demonstrates this uses stories such as this:

> Jo is sitting on a settee about to unwrap a chocolate bar. His mother says, 'Come on Jo, it's time for swimming'. He quickly places the chocolate bar under the cushions on the settee and goes off with his mother. Just after they have gone his sister comes into the room to look for her teddy. Imagine her surprise when she finds the chocolate. She hides the chocolate bar behind the book case.
>
> When Jo comes home hungry for the chocolate where will he look?

To us the answer is so obvious that it does not seem worth asking. We expect Jo to look under the cushions on the settee where he left it. But up to the age of about five it very likely that children will say, 'he'll look behind the bookcase'. The children listening to the story know that the chocolate bar is now behind the bookcase so that is where they expect Jo to look. To know that Jo will look under the cushions on the settee means that we understand Jo's intentions and beliefs. To be able to put yourself in someone else's shoes, to understand what someone else is thinking and feeling, is one of the most mysterious things that human beings do.

At this point you might want to go back to Task 5.1 (see page 64) to try one of the tasks as a teaching opportunity rather than as a test. What do you think might happen?

Children's social development

Piaget also investigated children's social development, their social learning. He agued that pre-operational children's understanding about the feelings and emotions of others can be limited because they are egocentric, they see the world from only their own point of view. They are, he suggested, unable to recognise that there may be other points of view. Jane came home very excited, 'Mummy, Mummy, there are three new girls today, they're twins.' Mummy listens and responds while Jane goes on to tell her all about the three 'twins'. After a while she gently says to Jane, 'Twins means two children Jane, but you're talking about three children?' 'Yes,' says Jane, 'three twins.' 'No Jane, two are twins and one is their older sister.' 'No Mummy, three twins.' Jane, like many small children, is at this point immovable on the 'three twin' issue. Piaget might explain this as not being able to see the difference between her own point of view (what is subjective) and what is actually correct (what is objective). To investigate this he used a model of a mountain and a doll. The task for the child is to pick a picture that shows what the doll sees. Very often children will pick the picture of what they see, not what the doll sees (Piaget and Inhelder,1956). Of course, there may be other simpler explanations about Jane's understanding: probably the word 'twin' is not yet linked to the concept of twin.

This view about children appears to be somewhat at odds with experience. It seems that Piaget took too simple a view about this aspect of development. It is clear that most children will recognise emotions in others and respond to them. At home the toddler sees that his carer is upset and says, 'Peter sad?' Peter, his child minder, says, 'Yes, Josh, I'm sad because …' telling him in simple terms that a friend had been hurt in a car accident. At which point Josh brings Peter his favourite toy as a gesture of sympathy. In nursery, the children react sympathetically when a pile of books falls on one of the helpers. Many teenagers seem happy to give their time to helping others. These sorts of observations have lead to work on 'theory of mind', or a set of ideas that explain the ways that we may understand how other people feel, their beliefs, ideas and behaviour.

What is intelligence?

One key question in cognitive development is to ask: what is intelligence? Piaget seems to have seen this as the child's total potential to learn. He appears to have taken the view that it is a unitary attribute – intelligence is intelligence.

Exploring ideas about intelligence, Howard Gardner (b. 1943) has given us some new ideas to think about (Gardner, 2001). He suggests that rather than being one thing, a unitary attribute, intelligence can involve many different aspects. His ideas about 'multiple intelligences' suggest that there may be many kinds of intelligences; obvious ones are those of music or maths, but what about people who are sensitive to the needs of others? Gardner suggests that this is a particular sort of intelligence, and he recognises many others as well. In the United States particularly, his work influences the ways that teaching and learning are designed from nursery through to higher education. Children and young people are encouraged to recognise and develop their particular intelligence. The idea has encouraged teachers to think about the ways that teaching can tap into different intelligences by using a variety of approaches to learning. Its impact is on developing a curriculum that allows for differences to be used and celebrated. Teaching may be tailored to allow for classes that group children with a particular intelligence. Children identified as having a musical intelligence will be encouraged to use this. There will be specialist input for children with physical intelligence, and so on. However, his ideas are not intended to endorse over-specialisation; general intelligences and abilities such as empathy are also to be promoted in teaching. Teachers and teaching teams who understand Gardner, whilst allowing for particular talents, will also encourage children to achieve their potential.

Information processing

Cognitive development theorists are increasingly interested in the analogy between a computer program and human learning. Information processing, or the rules for making decisions, has been a particular focus. The way a child changes and develops seems to be rule-bound. In language development, a question for investigation might be: 'How and when do children come to master the past tense?' If this could be reduced to a series of yes/no answers, like a switch which is either on or off, then we might know what the 'rules' in our brains are for 'doing the past tense'. I place information processing theory into the constructivist category because it seems to me that it is about the individual's approaches to learning.

One explanation put forward to suggest why some children seem to fail at Piagetian tasks is not that they do not understand them, but that they cannot recall the answers. Clearly this is an area that teaching teams have an interest in.

We have all thought we have successfully taught something only to find the very next day that no one remembers any of the important information. The idea that there may be memory stores which deal with what we need to know in different ways is intriguing and helps to explain why we both remember and forget. The way that the mind works in recalling information has direct relevance to teaching and learning. The link between the amounts we can hold in our working memory and cognitive development helps us to understand why adults can do certain things that children have yet to understand. A mental arithmetic problem that has two parts, such as $4 + 5 - 2$, requires us to hold both parts in the working memory, to note that there is a plus sign and a minus sign to deal with, and to recall from the long term memory the strategies that each of these signs requires. We must apply the strategies correctly, deal first with one and then the other, do the working-out, remember the answer to the first bit in order to work out the second bit. The opportunities for not being able to recall either information or processes at any stage in trying to reach the answer are considerable (Brainerd,1983; Case 1985). As the child's memory is still developing, what adults may consider a simple sum can be a step too far. But, in order to develop both memory and cognition, the learner needs exposure to such tasks. Many chances to try out a variety of strategies to solve problems and then to select consistently the one that best fits seems to be one way of assisting the development of memory and cognition.

Implications for teaching: constructivism

Cognitive development theory, as proposed by Piaget, has been much revisited and re-tested. Clearly learning and development are not as smooth nor as continuous as Piaget expected, and his theory has limitations as children can often do far more than it predicts including in competence in social interaction. However, features of Piaget's theory are still important to us. His influence and the work on information processing has been extremely important, leading to 'child/learner-centred' approaches to learning particularly for younger children, and to the development of the maths curriculum in the primary years and science in secondary schools. The idea that children, indeed all learners, construct both knowledge and the ways of working that they need is widely acknowledged in teaching teams.

Most would agree that at home, in early years settings and play areas, the young child is active and very often independent when playing. The child sets the agenda for play, he or she decides what to do and how to do it, and how much of it to do. The adult may be allowed to join in, may be told 'go away', may be asked for 'stuff', or the child may find things for him or herself. The child is in charge. The move to school may halt this independence. The child moves to a setting where he or she is one amongst many and where there are expectations about the sort of learning that is required. But in many classrooms, whilst there may not be as much opportunity to express individuality as there is at home, there are likely to be rich, well resourced indoor and outdoor spaces. The early years staff will be keen to allow for individuals to make choices about tasks. The tasks that teachers select will be varied. There will be a shared excitement about learning between children and those who support their learning.

Piaget's legacy invites us to think about the learner's needs, to begin to see learning from the novice's viewpoint. Where constructivism is used in classrooms, there is a voice for the learner in what and how they learn and projects are tailored to individual needs. The emphasis will probably be more on process than knowledge and teaching is about helping the learner to learn through the teacher making fine adjustments to tasks.

Following constructivist ideas, in curriculum areas such as maths and science the sequences of experience, which are linked to practical tasks and experimentation, are clearly established teaching strategies. At the same time the learning will be carefully ordered and structured to meet individual needs. Teaching teams strive to extend understanding through carefully listening and responding to the commentary that an individual makes about learning. Learning is not exclusively about the right answer but the way that the learner suggests a range of possible solutions; the wrong answer is seen as offering further teaching opportunities.

The teaching strategies that help children and young people to remember are another aspect of constructivism. Chunking (grouping ideas in order to be able to better learn or remember them) is a technique that to helps to fix ideas (Miller, 1956). We often use it to remember telephone numbers when we chunk numbers into two or three sets, either 26-74-19 or 267-419, in order to learn them. It is probable that this would be used in working out the sum discussed earlier (4+5−2). Several other teaching strategies for assisting memory may be familiar to you, including:

- imaging – where the learners are asked to create a mental picture (imagine yourself being able to ...);
- rhyming schemes (this would include learning the alphabet to a song tune like

Twinkle, twinkle little star);

- peg words – connecting things to particular words (one – bun, two – shoe);
- method of loci – connecting the things to be remembered to particular locations (use a journey round where you live to connect items to be remembered to particular rooms);
- acronyms – in education these can vary from the obscure to the familiar, (NEET i.e. Not in Education, Employment or Training, DHT i.e. Deputy Head Teacher).

CHAPTER 6

BIG theory 3: Vygotsky and social constructivism

Learning for Piagetian constructivists can be a solitary activity, but for another group of cognitive development theorists it is a social activity. Vygotsky and his followers suggest that learning happens where there are groups: a family, a class, or the workers in the supermarket. Furthermore, for Vygotsky instruction is an essential element of learning. This chapter introduces Vygotsky's theory and considers how it is used:

- Vygotsky's theory
- Implications for teaching: social constructivism

What is social constructivism?

Rather than the construction of knowledge being a solitary activity, Vygotsky argues strongly that individuals learn most effectively in groups. Learning, he suggests, is a social activity hence the term social constructivism.

Vygotksy's theory

Piaget's idea that the child learns and develops with little or no help is one that is totally rejected by Vygotsky. As a Soviet citizen living in the USSR, Lev Vygotsky (1896–1934) was virtually unknown outside his own country until his work began to be translated into English in the 1960s. His ideas, once available beyond Soviet Russia, changed the way that we think about learning and development. He makes us ask questions about what the adult's role is in children's learning, and it is because of his work that we have come to think that the way adults deal with children and young people can make a difference to their learning. A lawyer by training but fascinated by the study of language and other social sciences, Vygotsky was from 1924 onwards researching thoroughly all the available evidence about learning and development. His theory has four main ideas; children construct their own knowledge, development happens in social settings, learning helps development to happen, and language and being able to think cannot be separated.

Not surprisingly, for social constructivists play is seen as central to learning and development in the early years. Vygotsky identified features in play which suggest that he saw it not as free for all, but organised and rule bound. When children and young people play together they follow rules, they organise the play to suit their development needs. And, of course, the play of adolescents is quite different to that of young children.

When previously describing Piaget's theory, I told you the story about the toddler trying to work out whether what she was seeing was a sheep or a dog. She said over and over again, 'Not sheep, not dog; not sheep, not dog'. In Vygotsky's theory this is an example of *private speech*. In this theory some help should be given to the toddler to help her to construct a new understanding. I suppose an adult might have asked a series of questions; 'What can it be? How is it like a sheep? How is it like a dog? Do you think it barks?' Certainly in more formal settings this is what Vygotsky would expect the adult to do. Learning is helped and supported, or mediated, by a more experienced person. In this story that would be someone, not necessarily an adult, who knows the difference between a dog and a sheep and who can help the toddler make this distinction. One way we learn is through instruction, by someone helping us to understand and asking us to demonstrate that understanding.

Another way we learn is by imitation. Before baby is talking one thing parents may notice is that they hear noises that sound remarkably like speech. Baby, before dropping off to sleep, may seem to make noises that are speech-like. The words are not clear but the rise and fall in pitch, the pauses, the tone, all seem to sound like the conversation that the baby is hearing during the day. This observation suggests that the baby is imitating what it sounds like to be able to talk. Imitation may be beginning to fix this learning in such a way as to bring actual speech closer. You can see this in many school learning tasks; young writers often imitate the stories they know best or, in science, copy what the teacher does in the experiment.

Box 6.1 Four ideas that underpin Vygotsky's sociocultural theory

Children construct their own knowledge

This is a central idea for all cognitive theorists. They reject the behaviourist idea that learning is a result of the stimulus being reinforced. Both Piaget and Vygotsky agree that children are active in exploring their own worlds. For Vygotsky this is empiricist theory, whilst Piaget takes the nativist stance. Piaget takes the view that heredity plays a great part in development, whereas for Vygotsky what happens at home and school is more important that what we are born with; he thought the environment was most important.

Development happens in social settings

How and where you are brought up influences who you are. Russian children will of course all have different home lives than each other. But their home experiences or cultures will have much more in common than say that of American children brought up in American homes. Further, Vygotsky suggests that the quality of the child's home is an important factor in his or her development. We probably take this idea for granted, which might explain why we are so shocked when we hear of children being neglected.

Learning helps development to happen

For Piaget the child learns in stages; for Vygotsky learning is continuous – changes are made step-by-step and everything we experience has an effect on our development. Miss out a step in the learning, and the development may not be as sound as it could have been.

Language and being able to think cannot be separated

I am making ice cream using a new recipe. I gather the ingredients and the equipment, while in my head I am instructing myself, 'first do this, then do that, what did the recipe say about salt?' As adults we are probably only aware of private speech, the talk that goes on in our heads, when we are doing a task that is unfamiliar and needs our full attention. Vygotsky's view is that we should hear learners' private speech, that it is to be encouraged as a way of encouraging development.

Yet another way we learn is in groups and from each other. When children and young people are set tasks that require them to cooperate and work with each other to reach a solution this is a Vygotskian principle in action.

Vygotsky understood learning as an activity which arises from the settings in which it takes place. If you are a Russian then your learning and what you do will arise from this; the same goes for being American, English, Pakistani or Chinese. Each family group will have its own ways of rearing children and young people. Going to school is an important learning experience where the child will meet different people and meet new things.

A final idea from Vygotsky is the zone of proximal development (ZPD). If we use ZPD we keep tasks within but slightly above, what the child is currently able to do. It would only be worthwhile helping the toddler to understand that what she was seeing was a large white dog if this was within her ZPD. If she was not yet able to learn this construct, helping would not do the trick. However, if we did not try to help her get that understanding we would not know whether she could get to 'it is a large white dog' or not.

Implications for teaching: social constructivism

Jerome Bruner (b. 1915), like Vygotsky, is convinced that schools change children and young people. Reflecting on Vygotsky's writings, Bruner (1999) says some important things about learning in school. Learning, he suggests, is about experiences: doing things, hearing stories, meeting new ideas, getting to know about yourself and others. He thinks that rather than learning being a once and for all experience, we need to do some learning, then return to it to do some more. The skills, concepts and content taught in schools needs to be constructed in ways that let the learner visit and revisit the experiences. The spiral curriculum may seem commonplace to us but it is a very powerful tool in helping learning.

Social constructivists are interested in how children and young people learn. In social constructivism guidance from a leader, usually an adult but sometimes an older child working with younger children, is an essential role. The expert is expected to help the learning along for the novices. Language is seen as central to all learning. Probing questions, careful listening and the offering of information characterise social constructivists' attempts to share the learning experience with learners. Group discussion and group decisions also feature in learning and in the ways in which discipline is managed. With younger children, 'in our classroom we …' will be one of the phrases you will hear. School staff and the

Task 6.1 Design a teaching task using Vygotsky's ideas

You are asked to plan and deliver an activity to help to meet a specific learning objective. Plan for a group of six children who are familiar to you. Think of any recent teaching sequence that is similar to the learning objective below which is to blend three-letter words: for example, something that is apparently straightforward, a spelling activity or a number or science activity.

How would you move the learner from your maximum support, to some support, to the group taking control? These are key Vygotskian stages.

Refer to the example that follows to write your own lesson plan. You can make the lesson plan interesting by including some of the things which occur when we go on a learning journey with children and young people. This is an exercise in fiction but nevertheless your lesson plan will make an interesting contrast to mine. Here are some points to structure your lesson plan:

1. What would you do first? What do you need to know about each learner's knowledge about the learning objective?
2. How would you check their knowledge?
3. How would you check their ability to do the learning?
4. What would the learning objective be for Session 1?
5. What would your teaching approach be – what will your learners actually be asked to do?
6. How would you measure progress after Session 1?
7. How would you use the information to inform Session 2
8. Repeat steps 4–7 as often as you think you need to. How many sessions in all would you predict you might need?

I was asked to plan and deliver an activity to help children's ability to blend sounds. Learning objective: blending three-letter words. Resources: large letter cards; a p t n m r j h. Target words: pat, hat, mat; nap, tap, map; ham, jam, ram; pan, jam, tar. This is what I did.

Session 1: A group of six seven year old children are having a fun time learning to blend letter sounds. To start the task I have some letter cards large enough for everyone to see with 'p', 't' and 'a' on

➤

them. Each child in turn is asked to name the letter and its sound. Their initial responses to this task are noted. The next step is for three children to stand with the letters in the right order to spell the word 'tap'. Between them, with some help from the helper, the children sort this out. At this stage they are in a line with the letters in the right order, but there is about three paces between each child. The letters 't' and 'a' are moved closer together with all the children saying the sound for 't' and 'a' until 'ta' are linked – the children saying 'ta' and the letter children linking arms. Next 'p' is moved to make 'tap'. Repeat with another group of three children with a consonant, a vowel and a consonant. Check on each child's learning. End session. (N.B. There are some differences in the possible approaches to this task. One way is a + t = at, p+at = pat; another is p + a = pa, pa + t = pat. I prefer the second as it encourages the left to right scan but others have strong views that it should be the first approach.)
Evaluation: Jh, Ja, K and S can do this, probably without my help. P and L are unsure about letter sounds.

Session 2: Just P and L playing hunt-the-letter-sound bingo with all the letters.
Evaluation: J and P better at the letter sound correspondence.

Session 3: With all six children, repeat Session 1 with less input and all the letters.
Evaluation: Supported J and P but gave the others their chance to discover how many words they can make with the letters.

Session 4: How many words can you make? My role is to watch and praise but not to help. Use non words like 'raj' to discuss reading for meaning. (Can you have 'raj' in a sentence?)
Evaluation: Need to check that all the children can apply this skill when reading. Do this within three days.

Is my approach consistent with Vygotsky's theory? How does yours differ? What advice would you give me? What changes would you make to your plans?

children's friends will be seen by learners as people who can help their learning. If you remember, Luke got the help he needed with spelling from a family friend who enabled him to become much more self sufficient and self confident about this aspect of his learning. However, working together does not mean that working on your own is not valued. The teacher is also expected to stand back and encourage individual independence in learning.

This teaching sequence will be familiar: we establish what is known, move the learner on to a new idea and, when this is established, require them to transfer what they now know to try a new but related task. Using ZPD (zone of proximal development) is a familiar part of teaching. Suppose we had found the right moment for the toddler in the 'not sheep not dog' story to learn in this way. There would be three stages in the sequence. The first would be for the adult to do most of the thinking, structuring this for the child; asking: 'what are dogs like?', 'what are sheep like?' This is scaffolding for the child's learning. The second stage would be for the toddler to begin to work out the answer: 'dogs have four legs', 'sheep have four legs'; 'sheep go "baa, baa"', 'dogs go "woof"'; 'dogs have hair', 'sheep have wool'. Until perhaps there is an 'ah ha' moment when she gets it: 'four legs, goes woof, has hair = dog not sheep'. The final stage would be for the toddler to make more decisions when faced with a similar problem – when looking at a hang glider, answering questions about: 'is it a bird/is it a plane?'.

Table 6.1 *Stages in ZPD*

Stage	Who does what
1	Adult does most of the cognitive work
2	Learner and adult work together to solve problems
3	Learner thinks and solves problem without help

As you learn, you develop, and as you develop, you learn – though exactly how this relationship works in not clear. Getting the right help at the right point, and in the right amount, will mean that the learner can move on to the next learning. Judging that moment, when and what to do, is what competent adults do all the time in the home with their own children. This is what adults in settings beyond the home also do for learners.

Learning is a social activity. Teaching is not confined to adults: a child may support another child, 'this is how I do it', and help can come from a brother, sister or another child at playgroup – the possibilities are endless. The support may

Table 6.2 *Theories in the classroom*

Approach to learning Locus of control	*Control* Behaviourism External	*Guidance* Constructivist Internal	Social constructivist Internal
Goals	Teachers/teaching assistants make learning happen	Teachers/teaching assistants support individuals through stages of development	Teachers/teaching assistants guide learners so that they can forecast how well they will do on tasks, will know what they understand about tasks, will know what aspects of the task they can already do
View of learning	Focus is on similar curriculum delivery for all	Focus is on an appropriate curriculum for individual learners	Focus is on an appropriate curriculum for individual learners
	Teachers/teaching assistants make the judgements about progress	Shared judgement about progress	Shared judgement about progress
	Teachers/teaching assistants decide how tasks are to be undertaken	Learners have ideas about how they approach particular tasks	Learners have ideas about how they approach particular tasks
	Learners rely on teachers/teaching assistant's rewards and punishments	Learners have some ideas about their success on tasks Learners have a say in what and how they will learn	Learners have some ideas about their success on tasks
	Teacher/teaching assistant tells, learner does	Learning may be independent of teaching	Learners have a say in what and how they will learn
View of learners	Likely to get things wrong, lazy, in need of a strong hand, passive	Active scientist	Will do the work and conduct themselves well *if* they see the point
Adult's status Methods	The boss Rewards and punishment	The organiser or provider Individual support	The leader Acknowledgement, problem solving, support, talking things through, action planning

Adapted from Porter, 2003: 18.

be given just because it feels like the right moment. The idea of ZPD is important, knowing what you know and what you need to know is helped along by the leadership of others. Teaching teams have to know what they are teaching to make the match between what the learner knows and what the next piece of learning is.

Summary: theories in the classroom

Chapters 4–6 have introduced three major theories about learning and development. The main features of the three BIG theories as they work in classrooms are summarised in Table 6.2 (see page 80). I am indebted to Louise Porter for the short-hand terms 'control' and 'guidance': **control** nicely summarises the behaviourist theory, whilst **guidance** provides one word for the concepts and ideas about constructivism and social constructivism (Porter, 2003). The summary in Table 6.2 uses her framework, extending it by beginning to show how theory informs teaching.

Most of us believe that some things are within our control, and some things are not. This idea is known as **locus of control**, which is often referred to as just 'locus'. In some settings locus is external, that is, we are told what to do. In others it is 'internal', coming from within the learner.

We can think about approaches to learning through considering **goals** or aims. Following one theory, a teaching team might impose the goal of making learners be polite to each other. To do this they might impose a rule about saying 'please' when asking for something and they might enforce the rule with a reward. In another theory, the goal might be encouraged by discussing 'good manners', why they are important and agreeing on a set of principles to be used. Every theory we put into practice promotes a **view about learning** and, from that, a **view about learners**. The teaching team may think you have to *make* learners act politely or that they can be *encouraged* to do so. Either learners need to be directed or they need to be encouraged. Or the learner may discover that acting to help others aligns with what he or she wants to do.

The **status** of the teachers and teaching assistants is probably that of boss. As boss they have the right to tell learners what to do. The alternative is that they might choose to act as leaders, leading or guiding learners to achieve a shared goal. **Methods** are about how we act, what we do to get goals into place. Teachers and assistants might notice and reward all acts of correct behaviour and/or punish when the rules are ignored.

Finally try Task 6.2, applying the theories introduced in Chapters 4–6 to the stories provided.

Task 6.2 What would you have done? Applying BIG theory

Read the stories below. If you were the adult in each story what would you have done?

A group of five year olds have been set a maths task. They are asked to build a brick tower for each number on the work card. On the table are suitable bricks to make the tower and a set of stand-up number cards to show how many bricks are in each tower. For example, on the work card the target number might be two, so the child builds a two brick tower and finds a stand-up number 2. The work is supervised by an adult who provides appropriate feedback: 'Well done, that's a two brick tower and you've labelled it with a 2'. Three out of the four children quite happily get on with the task. Soon brick towers begin to appear all over the table. James, however, completely ignores the task; what he does is to build the highest tower he can. He has subverted the task set by the teacher. The adult checks to see if he has understood the task. He has, it's just that he has chosen not to do it. He knows perfectly well that what he is doing may well get him into trouble. He is prepared to take the risk of punishment to do the self chosen task.

Did you decide to:

1. Stop James, reminding him about the task? If you decided on this course, how would you have stopped him? What would you have said and done? What theory were you applying?
2. Ignore James and concentrate on the other children's learning? Why would you make this decision? What theory were you applying?
3. From the decisions outlined in 1 and 2 which feels most comfortable for you?

If you work with older children try this story.

You are supervising a group of twelve year olds on their first day in secondary school undertaking a construction task. They have to use

➤

newspaper and pins to build the highest structure they can. Sharika, however, is using the newspaper to make an elaborate boat. She has subverted the task set. You check to see if she has understood the task. She has, it's just that she has chosen not to do it. She knows perfectly well that what she is doing may well get her into trouble. She is prepared to take the risk of punishment to do the self chosen task.

Did you decide to:

1. Stop Sharika, reminding her about the task? If you decided on this course, how would you have stopped her? What would you have said and done? What theory were you applying?
2. Ignore Sharika and concentrate on the others' learning? Why would you make this decision? What theory were you applying?
3. From the decisions outlined in 1 and 2 which feels most comfortable for you?

 # Further reading Chapters 4–6

Bigges, M.L. and Shermis, S.S. (1999) *Learning Theories for Teachers* (6th edn.). New York: Longman.
This is a super book and it is not just for teachers, we can all dip into it for excellent information about the impact of theory on the things that we do day to day. Chapter 5 on Skinner repays very careful reading as it extends the brief introduction to operant conditioning provided here.

Keenan, T. (2002) *An Introduction to Child Development.* London: Sage.
Pages 24–6 provide more general information about behaviourism, and pages 147–9 offer an explanation of language development, comparing Skinner with other theorists. Chapter 6 provides a general introduction to cognitive theory.

Smith, P.K., Cowie, H. and Blades, M. (2005) *Understanding Children's Development* (4th edn.) Oxford: Blackwell.
Chapter 12 provides an excellent explanation of Piaget's theory. Chapter 13 deals with information processing and Chapter 15 extends ideas about Vygotsky.

CHAPTER 7

Managing learning

What can we do to make a difference? This chapter is about how we support learning and how we manage learning.

- What is learning?
- Making choices about managing learning
- Longer term outcomes
- What do we do to help learning?
- Views about learning

What is learning?

Learning is about long lasting change, it is about what we know and understand and can do, our likes, dislikes and all those things that make us who we are. When thinking about learning, the debates in psychology around nativism and empiricism are not easily worked out. Clearly some of the ability to learn is genetic. Sometimes the genetic element in learning is considered more important or even all important. At other times particular experiences that enable us to learn may be more prominent. The kinds of attention for children and young people that are provided by parents and carers at home, and teaching teams in school, can provide situations in which learning can flourish.

Considering the nativism versus empiricism argument, learning to talk clearly shows that both what we are born with, our genetic inheritance, and the support from parents and carers in our environment, have a part to play. Because all babies seem to make similar sounds from birth the assumption is that we are all born with the ability to learn any language. All babies babble and coo and, on the whole, adults find this irresistible: we really like listening to them and giving them attention. Bee and Boyd (2004) report that even deaf babies, using their hands, sign babble. This can be taken as evidence for the nativist position. Yet the fact that we learn to talk in our native tongue provides evidence for the empiricist position: if we are brought up in a Welsh speaking home, then our first language will be Welsh.

Like much of the learning that goes on in the home, babies learn to talk without much in the way of obvious effort from either baby or parents and carers. The baby coos and the carer coos back; the baby makes a sound, 'da, da' and the listener responds with 'dada, where's daddy?'. This seems to be a profitable experience for both parties. On the whole, children learn to talk, sit, walk, run, feed themselves and many other things without too much help; this is intuitive learning. When we set out to teach children or when anyone chooses to learn something, this is deliberate learning (Fox, 2005). Outside the home, in school, usually learning changes from being intuitive to something much more effortful; as learning to write requires more effort than learning to talk – it is deliberate learning. In our own lives when we choose to learn we know that effort will be required. We know that not everything we do in order to learn will be to our liking nor will it always be easy.

Intuitive learning bubbles away under the surface all the time. We do not stop to consider this learning, we just do it. Intuitive learning happens in different ways. Here are some:

- We pay attention to the sensory inputs we need and learn to ignore the others. The subtleties of our senses and perception mean that what seems loud to one person seems normal to another. This is perceptual learning and habituation.
- We use imitation to learn in our everyday life. One toddler says, 'just so', exactly mimicking the play group leader's way of speaking, even so far as to use a dialect and tone of voice that are distinctively different from her normal speech. Look at a group of young people on a night out to see how they imitate each other in all sorts of ways: in dress, movement on the dance floor and in their talk.
- Throughout life we use association to learn. Even very young children soon work out that if you are asked to put your boots on you are going to the park, boots = park. They soon catch on to associations between events.

- We try things out, keeping what works, to solve problems. Charlie found that if he threaded string between three of his cars he could take them all for a walk at the same time; he solved his problem informally. As children play they solve problems all the time, and in adult life we continue to use our intuitive learning to try to solve problems. How many of us have plunged straight into putting together flat-pack furniture, only later looking at the diagrams for help? In school, intuitive problem solving can lead to faulty learning. This is one reason why it is important to check how the learner arrives at the answer, not just whether the answer is right or wrong.
- Often we just know what to do: how to make friends, how to calm an upset child, when to be cross with someone, how to thread a needle or kick a ball to the right spot. We all use our intuitive learning, doing what comes naturally.

Deliberate learning also takes place at home. There are family traditions, habits and ways of doing things that are carefully passed on by parents and carers to their children. Children can ask for help too, they can choose to engage in deliberate learning. Alicia has just realised that she can tell the time. She has been working at this for about seven weeks and was keen to learn. Her brother, tired of telling her the time, was all for it and several of her friends can tell the time. Her Mum and Dad have promised a proper watch once she can tell the time. They helped by making extra sure that she saw what the clock settings were for going to school, meal times and bedtimes. What seems to have made a difference for Alicia was spotting when her favourite TV programmes were going to be on and matching these to what the clock showed.

In an older age group Sean at 14 was keen to know how to persuade the girl he liked to go out with him. Samantha, who he had known through infant and junior school, was his chosen confidante. Her advice was given not face-to-face – this was perhaps much too much like asking for help – but through a series of text messages. Sam mentored him through to the first date. This might be best understood as deliberate learning; certainly Samantha, as the mentor, showed considerable insight as to how relationships are built.

Making choices about managing learning

Think about Task 6.2 (pp. 82–3) in which you were invited to decide on the teaching strategy that you might have used with James. James had decided to do what he wanted to do, building a high tower and ignoring the set task. The issue

Task 7.1 'I know that now'

- Alicia could tell the time – she understood and could do this to the nearest five minutes.
- Jamil learned to clap in time to the music.
- Fatima learned to count to 100.
- Frank learned to hide when his Mum shouted.

Think about a 'I know that now' moment in your own experience. What made you able to do the learning?

1. Can you give a reason for wanting to be able to do 'it'? Alicia didn't want to miss her favourite TV shows. Jamil loves to drum and wanted to join in with his brothers' music-making. Fatima wants to play school with her sister, she likes to be the teacher. Frank knows that his mother might hit him.
2. What support was needed to learn? Who helped? How was the help given? Alicia was helped by all the adults who knew that she wanted to learn to tell the time. They said things like: 'School in five minutes', 'Ten to six, let's watch …'. Jamil's dad spent ages clapping with him. Fatima learned to count with her Grandma's help. Frank was taught fear by his mother.
3. What made you able to say, 'I know that now'? Gradually Alicia found that she was telling other people, 'It's time for school, it's 8.35'. Jamil's brothers invited him to their rehearsals. Fatima sat her little sister down and taught her 'one, two, three'. Frank – well actually, I don't want to tell you what happened to Frank. I'm sure you can imagine.

Commentary

All the learners, except perhaps Frank, undertook learning to fulfil their own needs. They engaged in learning tasks to meet inner needs. They were engaged in deliberate learning, seeking and accepting help from whoever was able to give it. And, in these tasks, they were successful learners. This success may help to build an ability to try again when inner needs are harder to meet. Frank's story is extreme and contrasts with the others. It is included to remind us that while we will find ways of coping, we can learn to be fearful. Some parents care for their child using very harsh control. Aligning learning to a child's, or any learner's, inner needs is clearly something that helps.

seems to be that the deliberate learning he was asked to do was being ignored. Common sense suggests that we should stop him and get him to do the set task. This is often the instinctive solution offered to the story. Adults, teachers, teaching assistants, parents and carers often say something like: 'He's got to do the set task, I'd tell him to get on with it'. This is often coupled with the reason: 'He's got to do the same task otherwise it's not fair to the other children'. This response suggests that we see ourselves as 'in charge', so we need to get James to do the task. 'OK, James, make this number now', would probably be enough to achieve this. James is an agreeable child, and he is likely to do as he is asked. If we think the locus of control is external to James, possibly he is being naughty. We are the ones making learning happen, we have set the task and we are in charge. It begins to feel as though the approach to learning is about control.

Sometimes adults give a different solution; their instinctive response is to leave well alone. If the view is taken that James is being an active scientist, and if the role of the helper is understood as providing the support to enable him to learn, then we could consider this to be using the guidance approach to learning. But the choice to ignore James's off-task behaviour could be for any number of other reasons: there are other children needing attention or James can be difficult to manage.

Of course, a strict division between the two approaches to learning is artificial. Understanding the reasons for either decision is not simple. The instinctive insistence that James does the number task may be followed by the comment, 'he can build the tower later'. Discussion with those who respond in this way usually reveals that there will be a negotiation between adult and child. This begins to feel like a switch in the approach to learning from control to guidance. Likewise the adults who let James go on with building the tower are likely to point out that he will still have to undertake the task as set. For them it is just a matter of when, not if, the task is to be completed. This time the change in approach to learning is from guidance to control.

Actually what happened was that his teacher's advice to the adult volunteer was: 'Leave James, just ignore what he is doing'. Later, when talking this through, she pointed out that he was not interfering with other children and she knew that he could do the task. On this occasion she thought the volunteer helper's time was better spent supporting the efforts of the other children. She chose when and where to talk with James about what 'on task' means and why it is important. Also, she made sure that he went on to do the task later. This suggests that she was building a relationship with him and means that she worked hard to see what his needs are, as well as how the curriculum can be taught to him.

As Sharika is older, would the decision-making by the teacher have been along the same lines as for James? We might, I suppose, expect Sharika to be more aware of the need for deliberate learning. We might insist that the work is done at the same time as the other students, or we might let her fail to finish the task requiring her to do the work in her own time. The use of punishment is a clear option.

Whatever our decision is about James or Sharika we could argue that there is no difference in outcome because either way eventually the tasks got done: James does complete the number task and Sharika makes a high structure. Thinking about James's and Sharika's stories, it is clear that deciding which theory underpins the choices to be made in managing learning is not straightforward. If we choose to use a control approach, James would do the task at the same time as the other children. But if he does it later, as he would under a guidance approach, is the delay important? It really depends on the different beliefs and values held by the adults. Control approaches to learning place the power in the hands of the adult who chooses the learning tasks, the order in which tasks are done and when they are done. Children and young people must do as they are bid. Guidance approaches to learning, by contrast, give choice in the tasks, how and when they are done. If you felt strongly that James and Sharika should do the tasks when they were first asked, then consider whether you were opting for a control approach. If you felt that James should be allowed to meet an inner need by building a tower, and that the number task could be done later, then perhaps you are more inclined towards using the guidance approach to learning.

Guidance theorists, such as Dweck (1989), point out that we are all controlled from within. In a guidance approach to learning, feedback is designed to tell children what they are doing, supporting their internal needs. The adult, as the more experienced learner, provides information about success or failure on the number and the tower building tasks, commenting on the process as much as the outcome. In a control approach to learning the adult is concerned about achievement. The expected outcome will be that all the children in the group will work to gain the reward: that number towers labelled correctly get a 'well done', as do high paper and pin towers. This is sufficient reward for these children. Even then, their willingness to undertake the task cannot be attributed to the reward alone. It is just as likely that they may have found the task one that matched their internal needs. In thinking about these two approaches to learning, it is our understanding about our intentions that is central. It is not just about the words that we use, even though these are important. Being observant, listening carefully and finding the right phrases to move children and young people on in their learning is a skilled business. We need to be aware of the locus of control and know what to do about it.

Longer term outcomes

In managing learning, awarness of learners' self confidence and self esteem is important. These considerations bring us to the area of self knowledge. We can think well about ourselves, or badly, or somewhere in between. This is about both how we feel and how we act, and involves effort and performance. Goal theory is one way of thinking about what motivates us. In Box 7.1 Dweck's theory (1989),

---

Box 7.1 Learning or performance goals

Children with learning goals:

- choose challenging tasks regardless of whether they think they have high or low ability relative to other children;

- optimise their chances of success;

- tend to have an incremental theory of intelligence;*

- go more directly to generating possible strategies for mastering the task;

- attribute difficulty to unstable factors e.g. insufficient effort, even if they perceive themselves as having low ability;

- persist;

- remain relatively unaffected by failure in terms of self esteem.

Children with performance goals:

- avoid challenge when they have doubts about their ability compared with others;

- tend to be self-handicapping so that they have an excuse for failure;

- tend to see ability as a stable entity;

- concentrate much of the task analysis on gauging the difficulty of the task and calculating their chances of gaining favourable ability judgements;

- attribute difficulty to low ability;

- give up in the face of difficulty;

- become upset when faced with difficulty or failure.

*The more you learn the more you are able to learn.
(Dweck, 1989: 111)

Box 7.2 Thinking about Frank

Frank's ways are not pleasing to his mother. If they continue to battle it out at home, it is highly likely that in other settings he will be uncooperative, not likely to conform and not likely to learn. If we have to deal with Frank, we would have to think hard about how to get him to learn. If we choose to use control approaches with him, we are likely to find our efforts subverted. I think it is highly likely that even when punished, he is not going to act in a way that will enable him to learn. Indeed, some will argue that this will make him even less likely to conform. Even punishment for children like Frank is better than being ignored as the punishment itself become a reward because it gives Frank attention. The more rewards and punishments are used with uncooperative learners, the more likely it is that, instead of changing, their internal needs become more fixed. What seems, at first, to be common sense, turns out to be not such a good idea.

In Frank's case his mother, not deliberately you understand, but because she is unable to help herself, is driven into a frenzy by Frank's ways of going about things. Her inner needs do not align with his inner needs. This is an unhappy story. His actions provoke her; her answer is to make Frank frightened of her, but note he continues to adore her. How can we explain this? One view would be to say that in Frank's case the external control that his mother has over him is greater than his ability to meet his inner needs. If you think back to the ideas summarised in Box 4.2 (see page 57), you might conclude that this is operant conditioning and probably positive punishment. The patterns of behaviour that each have established are very strong.

It is possible to re-write this story. If his mother had been aware of guidance approaches this is how it might have gone for Frank aged five. Frank does something that his mother really finds awful, he crayons on the walls and not on the paper provided. His mother explains that she really would rather he does not do this, and then, this is important, gives him some alternatives. He can have a huge piece of paper to crayon on, he can have some smaller pieces of paper to crayon on, whatever. Frank offered a choice within his ZPD (introduced in Chapter 6), dithers for a moment, then opts for the big paper. Mother, rather than leaving him unsupervised, stays and talks with him about what he is doing.

Think what Frank might be like at age 12 if nothing is done to repair the relationship and re-educate both mother and child.

which contrasts learning goals with performance goals, helps us to understand this. She suggests that the tasks we set should incorporate information about how children and young people succeeded previously. She suggests that we tell them how well they did on similar learning in the past and talk to them about the effort that they are putting into learning, and we need to celebrate their successes.

It is possible that children and young people with either learning goals or performance goals will respond well to different approaches to learning. When they have learning goals they are much more likely to be able to meet the demands set by learning. They are the tryers in classrooms and they thrive on challenge. They respond well to the guidance approach to learning. They are likely to be self confident and to have high self esteem.

Perhaps children and young people with performance goals are much more likely to flourish under a control approach to learning. They are really keen on rewards. This leaves us with a problem, as perhaps we should help them to become more learning-centred because this may boost their self confidence and increase their self esteem.

There are questions to consider about the approaches to learning that we can choose to use when managing learning. If children and young people become reliant on being told what to do, when they are right and when wrong, does this make taking responsibility for learning more difficult? If we fall into a habit of mostly using control approaches with James, will it have a long-term effect on his learning? The downside to the control approach is that it may make children and young people too dependent on being told what to do. They may lose the ability to think 'outside the box', to solve problems for themselves, and limit their creativity. If ideas about learning for its own sake are important then adopting control approaches may be limiting. In the long term, as adults, they may find being flexible enough to learn new ways of working difficult.

What do we do to help learning?

As teaching teams we take the responsibility for the teaching that goes on. There is a curriculum to be delivered and our work is scrutinised to make sure that this happens. Whether we involve the learners or not, we are responsible for assessment and teaching. It our responsibility to know what it is we are teaching, to understand the concepts, processes and knowledge, to be clear about what is easy to learn and what is not. We know that making the tricky bits doable is what we have to achieve. We give children and young people feedback as they work on both their effort and success: 'You're working hard, that bit's right, have another go at this.' When they are successful, we let them know: 'You're clever at that.' We have to be accurate, knowledgeable, imaginative and aware about our learners' needs and abilities when managing learning.

Table 7.1 What do we do to help learning?

Teaching cycle	In **control approaches** to learning, teachers and teaching assistants take responsibility for:	In **guidance approaches** to learning, teachers and teaching assistants:
1. Collect data	• Finding out what learners know and can do	• Work with learners in finding out what they know and can do
2. Analyse data	• Deciding what learning is completed and what is not	• Help learners in deciding what learning is completed and what is not
3. Evaluate data	• Deciding on the next step in learning either for the individual or the group	• Make the final decisions about the learning objectives, but only after sharing the decision making on what the next step in learning is with either the individual or the group
4. Propose action	• Design and implement a suitable lesson	• Designing and implementing a suitable lesson

5. Use the cycle of teaching to evaluate concerns and issues arising from the lesson, consider available teaching strategies, try these out, find out whether a strategy worked and either keep it in the repertoire or try other strategies.

If we decide to use a control approach to learning then young people are expected to learn in ways that the adult decides and the steps that are needed to learn will be direct: 'do this', 'now this'. The teaching will be adjusted based on how well, or badly, learners do when tested.

In the guidance approach to learning the adult and learner are expected to work together, and with others in the group, to make decisions about how to go about learning. Learners are expected to:

• have some ideas about what they want and need to learn;
• predict how well they will do with tasks;
• know what they understand about tasks;
• know what aspects of the task they can already do.

One aspect of managing learning is thinking about the ways in which newly acquired knowledge can be transferred. Task 7.2 demonstrates this by inviting you to tie a bow tie. If you can tie your shoe laces this should be an easy problem to solve … however it seldom is!

Task 7.2 Using existing learning for new tasks

In many ways learning is invisible. It is hard to know what we know and harder still to decide what someone else knows. But if we are to help others learn, we have to find out what is known and what is not. Or more correctly, we need to help learners know what they know and what they do not know. We are dealing with deliberate learning which is often an effort and takes time.

In order to demonstrate this, think about why it is so difficult to tie a bow tie even though you can a shoe lace. After all it is basically the same task. I ask my students to do this. First they all demonstrate that they can tie a shoe lace. Then, without instruction, they are asked to tie a bow tie. So far I have only had one student who could do this straight away – he worked in a rather smart restaurant as a waiter. On the whole, in my classes most people cannot do it.

I set the learning outcome as a challenge. I make it clear that everyone should be able to tie a perfect bow tie. There is often a useful hook: the motivation of an end of year ball, to capture interest, and there is also a small prize – a box of chocolates. There is a chance to experiment with a bow tie and this is when they find that it is not that easy. At this point, we pair off to work out how to do the task. As the pairs talk about the task they discover what they know and understand and what they need to find out about which we draw up into a list. This includes finding out what a properly tied bow tie really looks like (these websites work well for this: www.tcf.ua.edu/bowtie/, www.bowtieclub.com/ > how to tie, www.formalwear.org/public/resources/bowtie.html). The boxes for ties have instructions as well, but even following instructions has its problems. Eventually, this usually takes a 15 minute slot over several sessions for one or two people to do it. At this point they become our experts, teaching others how.

➤

What can we learn from this?

Each learner has to make clear what is understood and what is not. I find that I often need to talk to find out what I understand and what I don't, and it sometimes helps to do this with more experienced people.

Each learner has to be able to recall what is understood: memory is an important aspect of learning. We may be able to rehearse tying a shoe lace by saying what it is we are doing. We might cluster the information we have about knots together, linking all the things that we know about tying. We might find a mnemonic, a memory trigger, for tying a bow. We might systematically search for everything we know about ties, bows, knots, fabrics, and anyone we know who might be familiar with bow ties.

Each learner has to be able to apply what is understood to new tasks. Being able to tie shoes laces is one step, tying a bow tie is a whole new task.

Teaching Strategies

We can use these strategies with learners:

- Discuss how to go about a task.
- Promote problem-solving strategies: 'have you done anything like this before?', 'what did you do? … could you try …?', 'what if …?', 'how about …'.
- Get learners to set targets: 'I'll spend five minutes each coffee break trying to tie a bowtie.'
- Make sure everyone is aware and understands what is to be learned and how the task might be done.
- Get learners to reflect on the mental strategies they are using: 'How did you do that? What did you do first? And then …?'
- Encourage them to talk accurately about how they are working things out. (Smith, 2001a; Adey, 1988)

Views about learning

If we take a control approach to learning then there are at least three likely results:

- Some learners will come to rely on you to tell them how to undertake tasks; they may not know how they learn.
- Because teachers and teaching assistants provide the judgements about how well children and young people perform on any task, they may not be able to self assess. They may not know whether their work has merit or not.
- As the power seems to lie very much with you, this may mean that learners have difficulty in telling you about what they know. As one eight year old said, 'It is the teacher who tells you what to do, and how to do it, so don't you ask me, just you tell me what you want me to do.'

The guidance approach to learning reverses these effects. Teaching strategies will include:

- guiding children and young people through the tricky aspects of learning, through coaching and mentoring;
- helping learners become really perceptive about their own learning: 'How well will you do?', 'How well did you do?', 'How are you going to do it?', 'How well did that way of doing it work?';
- giving learners a vocabulary to talk about their learning: 'I think I'll be able to do …', 'I expect to do well because …', 'I'll need help with …', 'I'm going to try doing that by ….'.

Summary

All learning is about change. It is about what we know and how we know it. We learn, probably most of the time, intuitively. Deliberate learning can be demanding. In this chapter, the approaches to learning have been contrasted as either guidance or control; however, most teachers and teaching assistants will use both, slipping seamlessly between control into guidance and back again. It seems to be a characteristic of human beings that we can hold and act on contradictory views. We can be both child-centred guidance approach users and control approach users. What is important is to know which approach we are using and why. We need to understand our own theory about learning.

 Further reading

Fox R. (2005) *Teaching and Learning: Lessons from Psychology*. Oxford: Blackwell Publishing.

Chapters 6 and 8 give a full picture about intuitive and deliberate learning and lead us to thinking about the ways in which we teach.

For work with secondary school students:
Capel, S., Leask, M. and Turner, T. (2005) *Learning to Teach in the Secondary School: A Companion to School Experience* (4th edn.). London: Routledge.

Overall, L.S. and Sangster, M. (2007) *Secondary Teacher's Handbook* (2nd edn.). London: Continuum.
These two practical books offer guidance in implementing the cycle of teaching (set out in 'How to use this book'), considering a range of teaching strategies.

For work with younger children:
Bruce, T. (2004) *Developing Learning in Early Childhood*. London: Paul Chapman Publishing.
Ideas about how adults support and help children and young people to learn are explored in some depth in this book.

Dweck, C.S. (1989) 'Motivation', in A. Lesgold and R. Glaser (eds) *Foundation for Psychology of Education*. Hillsdale, NJ: Laurence Erlbaum. pp. 87–136.
The chapter provides an introduction to Dweck's theory. For further reading see the following article and book.

Dweck, C.S. (1999a) 'Caution–praise can be dangerous', *American Educator* 23(1): pp. 4–9.
Dweck, C.S. (1999b) *Self Theories: Their Role in Motivation, Personality and Development*. Philadelphia: Psychology Press.

Riley, J. (ed.) (2001) *Learning in the Early Years: A Guide for Teachers of Children 3–7*. London: Paul Chapman Publishing.
A practical book that extends the theme of managing classroom learning.

Overall, L.S. and Sangster, M. (2007) *Primary Teacher's Handbook* (2nd edn.). London: Continuum.
Sangster, M. and Overall, L.S. (2006) *Assessment: A Practical Guide for Primary Teachers*. London: Continuum.
These practical books deal with a range of teaching strategies, necessary for putting into practice the cycle of teaching.

CHAPTER 8

Managing discipline

The BIG theories from Chapters 4–6 apply to the things that we do to manage children's and young people's conduct. Conduct or behaviour is about the ways that we act, the things we do to fit into a family, a school, at work and at play. It is also about our ways of working, including persistence, our ability to keep at it, and resilience which is the way we recover from setbacks. Discipline is about those things that we do to help individuals to manage their own conduct. Where there is no misbehaviour, no conduct that causes concern, there is no need for discipline.

Teachers and teaching assistants have an opportunity to get to know those who they teach really well. Working one to one offers a great opportunity to understand someone's inner needs. We begin to understand what makes him or her tick, how the child or young person learns. We begin to have ideas about what the individual learns, can learn and barriers to their learning. We also begin to form ideas about his or her conduct in our setting. We know what individuals can be like when they are working in groups, in whole class settings and in other parts of the school: the gym, dining room and yard.

We each have our own ideas about how we expect children and young people to conduct themselves where we work. How we expect children and young people to conduct themselves, to behave, and how they actually conduct themselves will either be a source of conflict or the beginnings of building a working relationship. This chapter considers:

- What do we mean by 'managing discipline'?
- Views about children and young people
- The outcomes of control and guidance approaches
- What do we do about social and emotional development?
- Do children and young people understand social behaviour?

- Learning from parents
- Our expectations about conduct
- Using control approaches
- Praise and blame
- Do control approaches work?
- Using the guidance approach

What do we mean by managing discipline?

At home the rules of relationships are often learned intuitively. The young child will have learned when to be noisy, when to be quiet, he or she may have a good idea about what annoys and what pleases relations and friends. The change from home to any new place can be a complex learning challenge for the child. What you learn in your first setting beyond the home may help decide what you do in the next class, school or out-of-school group. It is our ability to understand and adapt to the new that enables us to fit in.

If there is a good match between the way relationships between adults and the child work at home and at the playgroup, then going to playgroup will be straight-forward; the toddler is likely to fit right in. If at the playgroup the new child does not share an understanding about how to get along with other children and new adults, then there may be issues to sort out. Whether easy or smooth, the move from home to a new place is always going to lead to new social learning for those involved. This social learning continues as children get older and move from play-group to nursery to infant school and then to other new settings. Each transition challenges them with new experiences and the need to fit into new ways. What we learned about conduct from a previous setting may help us to fit in.

Making 'fitting in' easier for very young children leads to solutions like creat-ing a 'third space', somewhere that makes a clear link between home and the new setting. The third space is a place where what is valued at home – home cul-ture, religion, language and conduct – is brought into the setting. Early years workers let the children make a place of their own in the new setting (Cook, 2005). As we may be the first adults that children meet beyond the home, we need to be able to deal with the child on his or her terms. Visits by playgroup workers to the child's home in order to get to know the child's space, and by the child to the playgroup, are successful ways of bridging the gap and of making the transition a happy one.

It is easy for the child to get things wrong and not to understand how to act. After all, why should they know the ways to conduct themselves in the new setting? The child will use home learning about social rules at playgroup, that is what he or she knows best. Those who work with young children are sensitive to their needs for reassurance, especially when they are away from the familiar for the first time. Even when the fit between conduct at home and school is similar, the transfer from home to the new setting will need some help. This will be true about the transfers between schools as well – more opportunities to learn it is true, but also more opportunities to make conduct mistakes. Some older children and young people may need a great deal of help in understanding how to make the best use of their time in schools and colleges.

Views about children and young people

When children's conduct is not what is expected this may be seen as an issue: a child snatching a toy, or talking when others are quiet. We get annoyed with what children and young people do, not who they are. This distinction is important. It is the rule breaking that irritates. Whatever they do that breaks our notions about conduct we still need to value the child or young person as unique and special. The child's or the young person's ideas about conduct can conflict with adults' expectations. It is the things that the child or young person does, his or her actions, that makes the adult decide to change the behaviour.

What adults do when they step in, the kind of discipline that they decide to use, will reflect their views about children and young people. We can see them as likely to make mistakes which gives us an opportunity to work with them on self control, helping them to learn strategies that are appreciated as the right thing to do; to wait or ask for a toy, to know that the right thing to do is to be quiet when others are. This attitude follows the guidance approach to discipline. If we think that the learner has not understood or that they have made a mistake, then our use of discipline will be about helping him or her to learn what is 'OK', what is viewed as correct conduct. They will be helped to learn to ask for the toy and to learn the signs that mean that it is time to be quiet.

If, on the other hand, we see children and young people as naturally likely to misbehave, as 'naughty', it is more likely that there will be rules that if kept gain reward and if broken are punished. The learner is told what is acceptable. If he or she keeps to the rules then there will be rewards. If the rules are broken punishment happens. Taking the toy will mean that the child may not be allowed that toy at that point; being noisy when you should be quiet may mean being removed from the room. Asking for the toy will gain a reward, as will being quiet at the right time.

Of course, it is often not as simple as that. Most of us are not consistent in our reactions to events. On one occasion we may be tolerant about the child who snatches the toy and the noisy young person. We choose to ignore the conduct. On another occasion we may choose to work with the learner to develop his or her understanding about appropriate conduct. On yet another occasion we may find the child or young person very irritating; because we are busy we may need to use a more controlling approach, punishing the learner for breaking the rules. It is amazing how tolerant most learners are about our inconsistencies, in the variation in approach that we use. They seem to cope with our switches and mood swings quite well. Some children and young people do find us hard to understand though, so it is worth giving some thought to how consistent we need to be.

Task 8.1 What is misbehaviour?

1. In the art room, Darren (aged 13) is quietly working on a large painting. Passing by Louise nudges him, causing him to drop his brush on the floor. He is very annoyed, shouting at Louise, and in his anger drags the paint brush across his work.

Darren is out of order, this is misbehaviour. Has Louise also misbehaved? In this case the teacher who saw what happened thought not.

2. One of the teaching assistants reports the following story. The tale would be much more difficult to sort out if it had to be explained by the children involved.

It is a hot sunny day, Jack (aged 4) is outside using water and a paintbrush to paint the paving slabs. He is quietly occupied, doing his own thing. Sarah (aged 3), on her way from one place to another, walks across the paving slab that Jack is painting. He picks up his water pot and throws the water all over her. She cries and gets upset, he cries and gets upset.

Jack is out of order, throwing water over someone is misbehaviour. He is older than Sarah so should 'know better', but Sarah has also misbehaved by spoiling his game.
➤

Answer these questions. Use the theories about approaches to learning to support the actions that you suggest. You may wish to refer to Table 6.2 (see page 80) to refresh your knowledge about the theories.

1. In story 1, if you thought Darren was misbehaving, what would you do? What would you do with Louise?
2. In story 2 what would you do if you thought both children were naughty, that they had spoilt each other's games deliberately? What would you do if you thought Jack was naughtier than Sarah?
3. In story 2 what would you do if you thought both children had made mistakes which gave you a chance to work with both of them about being thoughtful about others?
4. In both stories what would happen if you decide to do nothing, other than drying Sarah off?

Some thoughts about the answers:

1. If you thought Darren was well out of order you might have imposed a punishment. What would be appropriate? Louise, in this case, apologised to Darren immediately. The teacher took no further action with Louise. Does using a control approach have any downsides in this story?
2. In story 2 if you think that both children have been naughty you would probably have:
   - Punished Jack and thought that Sarah had been punished enough by being soaked.
   - Used the incident to introduce two new rules. One about not throwing water, ever, and another about not walking through other people's games.

   Both these answers are entirely consistent with using the control approach to stop the behaviour.
3. In story 2 if you think that both children have made a mistake you will see it as an opportunity to set them both some activities to help them to learn from their mistakes. You will use the guidance approach. You would probably have:
   - Talked with each child separately about what happened and how it could be avoided.
   - Talked with them together about how to be friends.
   - Used the incident to work with all the children in the nursery about what 'being kind' means.
4. The option of doing nothing in story 2, or as little as possible, is totally ➤

appropriate if Jack, as soon as he has calmed down, apologises to Sarah. He acknowledges that he has made a mistake. You might still need to work with both children to give them strategies for dealing with similar events. This is entirely consistent with using the guidance approach to dealing with the children's mistakes

Doing nothing in story 1 might also be an option if Darren's anger is really directed against himself. If he apologises and puts things right then there would be no need to do anything.

The outcomes of control and guidance approaches to discipline

Either approach will claim self control or self regulation as an outcome, that the child or young person becomes more able to manage his or her own conduct. To decide which approach to use we need to think about the ways that the outcomes are achieved. As adults impose the rules and set the rewards and punishments, the control approach to discipline is more about compliance, getting children and young people to agree with the adult's point of view. They need to do as they are asked.

In the guidance approach to discipline, the child or young person is at the centre. This approach is really about developing their ability to make decisions about conduct for themselves. They need to make the decision to do as they are asked, or not. You will recall that in Task 6.2 (see pages 82–3) James decided to build a high tower rather than do the teacher's task and that his decision was honoured. His completion of the set task was dealt with in a way that recognised his inner needs. In the long term this approach may give learners a better chance to be adults who can self regulate. The young man who knows how to control his anger, young people who know how to resist pressure and how to be assertive, and who have clear ideas about what is right and what is not, are desirable outcomes.

What do we do about social and emotional development?

Our wider role is clearly important in this aspect of children's and young people's development. The places where we work provide a safe space outside the home where we can start to explore relationships. Children and young people need help in understanding their own behaviour and that what they do and the ways in which they act will be felt by others. They learn how to make and keep friends, how to resist doing the wrong thing and how to know what is the right thing to do.

Box 8.1 Social development

Learning to be a social being is extremely important. If we want a just society then we will see this as our job. Part of social development is about understanding concepts about gender, ethnicity, morality, citizenship and culture. By observing the influence of friends on those you work with, you will already know that the peer group has an effect on achievement. There is evidence that children and students need to be accepted by their peer group to do well at school (Rubin and Coplan, 1992; Wentzel and Asher, 1995). Social interactions develop alongside intellectual, linguistic and physical capabilities. Erickson (1963), a developmental psychologist, gives a framework for understanding social development, suggesting the stages that lead to self-sufficiency by adolescence. He suggests the need for a safe and secure environment to develop trust.

The milestones in social development are:
- Babies take an interest in other babies at about six months, they smile and make noises at each other. By one year some turn-taking can be seen.
- Between 12–24 months, infants play in *parallel*, that is, they play alongside each other rather than together. They start to become aware of a world beyond themselves, engaging in the rules that govern social exchange, for example, turn-taking in conversation, expressing empathy: 'Mummy sad' or 'Dad cross'.
- At three years *cooperative play* with turn-taking starts. When playing they start to know who to give in to and how to be in charge.
- Four years sees *associative play* with sharing play items. *Theory of mind*, being able to understand the position of someone else, which began much earlier, is now acquired. Fighting is a normal developmental stage and the cause of disputes are often soon forgotten.

➤

- Six year olds have more friends and enemies and play in bigger groups; fights and feuds are sorted out with less adult help.
- Seven–nine year olds work out how to 'do friendship', getting to know what they need to do to be accepted as peers.
- In adolescence friends become as or more important than parents for social support. Girls tell their best girlfriend(s) lots of things that their parents may not know. Choosing whom to associate with becomes an individual choice. Often these are same sex groupings with similarities in race, religion, similar academic and personality types. However opposites may also attract, as someone with complementary characteristics may be sought. Parents may not approve of the choice made.
- Early in teenage years boys, in particular, often form large groups with a shared interest, for example, music, football and clothing. These groups may dare to do things that, on their own, students would not attempt. The relationships within different contexts may be complex, with different groupings in different settings. As sexuality becomes important, adolescents begin to pair off. By the end of adolescence there are often couples with a smaller circle of like-minded friends.

Do children and young people understand social behaviour?

On the whole children seem to have quite clear ideas about conduct. This list of rules for the playground designed by five year olds shows that they know about social behaviour, that there are many things that you should not do. The children seem to favour the control approach. Here are some of their very long list of playground rules:

- Do not hit people
- Play nicely with your friends
- Do not play on the steps
- Do not go on the field when it is wet
- Put your rubbish in the bin
- Do not throw sticks or stones

- Do not climb on walls

The teacher, seizing the moment to deal with conduct beyond her well-ordered classroom, worked with the children to rephrase the rules to make them easier to keep. Together they reduced the list to these rules:

- Play nicely
- Keep hands and feet to yourself
- Stay in the infant yard
- Only throw balls
- Stay on the ground

The children and the teacher worked out the rewards for keeping to the rules and the punishments for breaking them. Is this the beginnings of a middle way? Clearly it is rule-based and is enforced by rewards and punishments, making it a control approach. At the same time the teacher is acting as leader, guiding children into making decisions about what goes on in the playground, which is what we would expect from a guidance approach. Sometimes control approaches are necessary but it seems important to use conduct mistakes as opportunities to move individuals towards self regulation.

There is a an idea, often confirmed by the media, that children and young people are out of control and that they do not know 'how to behave'. This may be true for some: there are children and young people whose conduct gives considerable cause for concern, however, there are many others who clearly have good self control. They know how to manage difficult events and they have learned to stand up for themselves without being unpleasant or violent. Like the young children with their playground rules, they have clear ideas about what to do and how to go about making 'right things' happen.

Learning from parents

Box 8.2 Approaches to parenting

You will note that the children phrased their playground rules as a series of 'do not' instructions. They might have got this from nursery and school staff. They might have got it from home. Here is some research about how parents ➤

manage their own children follows.

1. Do all adults fall into one of these patterns of behaviour when working with children? What do you think?
2. Which parenting type will be high on guidance with their children? Which will be high on control?
3. Does having knowledge about the way parents may deal with their children make a difference to how you will work with them (both the children and the parents)?

Parenting type

Permissive parent

There may be rules but they won't be carried through and the child might not know what they are. Children get attention and their way by crying, whining and nagging. Parent sometimes gives the child attention but sometimes dismisses him or her. There are no challenges for the child to behave in a more mature way. Any bad behaviour is ignored. Seldom cross or impatient with the child. There is warmth in the relationship between parent and child. 'Oh, he is alright, let him be' may be the response when the child is expressing himself/herself in an unrestrained way.

Authoritarian parent

There are rules and these are absolutely kept to but may not be well explained. Bad behaviour is dealt with and punished. Anger and displeasure will be clearly communicated to the child. The child is naturally naughty and has to be 'tamed'. Children's views are of no importance, and are not sought. There is not much warmth between parent and child. The child is not well understood. Little may be expected from formal education.

Authoritative parent

The rules are firmly kept and clearly explained. Bad behaviour is dealt with. Displeasure and annoyance are shown when there is bad behaviour. Pleasure is shown and there is support for good behaviour. Children have a voice and opinions which are listened to and may be acted on. High on

➤

warmth, involved and responsive to children. Age appropriate behaviour is expected. School and outings are important. High standards at school are expected.

Neglecting parent
Parent has limited relationships with children.

(Summarising, Baumrind, 1967, reprinted in Hetherington and Parke, 1993: 431 and expanded by Maccoby and Martin, 1983; Whiting and Edwards, 1992.)

Any adult who works with children can learn from the descriptions of parenting in Box 8.2. How parents deal with their children helps to explain why children and young people act as they do. We can expect the child of a neglecting parent to have developed ways of conduct that suit him or herself. As the adults at home are not interested, the child grows increasingly self reliant. This may serve very well at home, but there may be a real mismatch between the child's actions and the conduct expected in school. The children of permissive parents have learned that whining gets a result. They may be surprised when it does not work on you!

When considering the four parenting styles, most parents will admit to using all four, but mainly they aspire to being authoritative. I suppose in the way we behave as educators, we want to be closest to authoritative as well. We like to think we behave as a good parent would. However, as a worker with children and young people it is not enough to be an authoritative parent. Our authority should come from our expertise (Gordon, 1991). We have different responsibilities. Rather than just using parenting skills we need to act from a strong knowledge base. Authoritative parenting skills may form part of our repertoire, but we need to know much more than a good parent. In Task 8.1 (see pages 102–4) we need to know that Jack's loss of control is not unusual for four year olds and that what three year olds do is to move on in a straight line from one activity to the next. Our expertise includes knowing what we can expect from children and young people by understanding what social and emotional development we might expect at particular ages and stages. We need knowledge so we can make wise decisions when dealing with their mistakes. We should know how to think about what we do, to reflect and evaluate on the effectiveness of our actions. We need to use this thinking to decide which strategies to keep and which to change.

Box 8.3 Emotional development

Over time, children move from having others help them control their emotions, to being more able to do this for themselves. Some researchers suggest that emotional regulation goes on throughout life (Thompson, 1991). Individuals vary hugely in the amount of self-regulation displayed. Think of the ease with which some people you know can cry. Others seem unable to show any emotions. These aspects are closely linked to social development (see Box 8.1 page 105). Whilst early nurturing and differences in child care may make a substantial difference to emotional development, outside the home, friends and other adults including school staff and playworkers are influential.

Your influence is in the way in which you deal with those you work with. Your respect for them is important in their emotional development, and you have the opportunity to model how to be emotionally mature in the way you manage your work. You will have opportunities to recognise and discuss issues that have emotional as well as intellectual content: equity and equality, prejudice and fairness.

There are several areas of study that are associated with our understanding of emotion. One is temperament. You'll know the sort of person that you are: for example, you might 'be able to argue for England', or you might be easy going, taking everything in your stride. Your temperament is closely tied to your emotional type. Another area of study is the work on attachment between babies and parents. Early nurturing and differences in child care may make a difference to emotional development. These two aspects begin to explain why children may react differently in the setting where you work.

Being able to make judgements about another's feelings and emotional state develops from birth. Judgements about emotion are made on the continuum of happiness to sadness, the emotions of fear, anger, rage, guilt and shame. Through childhood into early adolescence an ability to understand how others feel becomes increasingly sophisticated. As the child's intellectual understanding develops, it seems that more than one emotion and the relationship between them become established. For example, eight year olds will say things like, 'I'm cross when I'm interrupted, but if it is to go out to play I'm happy' (see Box 5.2 on Theory of Mind, page 66).

Babies connect first with those who care for them. Adults reinforce the ➤

expressions that their six to eight week old babies make: smiles are met with smiles as facial expressions are used to monitor the supposed emotion. This seems to be the beginning of developing a range of emotions. The baby's smiles are gradually given more readily to the adults who make the most difference to him or her. Seven to nine month old babies show 'stranger distress', crying when strangers appear (Sroufe, 1996); the emotions of fear and anger also develop at about this time. Much of the display of emotion seems to be part of intellectual growth. There seems no doubt that toddlers learn, from the reactions of others, a whole range of emotions and how to show them. By age two, toddlers will switch from pouting to crying if it is to their advantage.

Our expectations about conduct

Our expertise means that we expect more from the older child Jack than the three year old Sarah-Louise (Task 8.1, pages 102–4). Our expertise also leads us to expect that there may be gender differences in the two children's responses, and to have ways of dealing with this. We are aware that their ability to understand the consequences of their actions will be different. We may expect girls to be more sensitive towards what is appropriate conduct and for boys to need a little more help with this aspect of their social development. We know that treating children fairly does not mean that we can deal with them in exactly the same way. We understand about their social, emotional and intellectual development. It is this knowledge, informed by theory, that provides a basis for the actions we take when teaching and working with learners, towards acceptable conduct.

Using control approaches

In many schools the approach to discipline follows the control approach, with the school staff using behaviourist theory to support their discipline. There are rules which are enforced through the use of rewards and punishments. You may well have met approaches such as Assertive Discipline (Canter and Canter, 1977) which uses reward for positive behaviour, or the ABC framework (Wheldall and Merritt, 1984) where the emphasis is on being consistent, using brief 'desist strategies' calmly, quietly and implacably. In passing, note that the ABC approach arises directly from Skinner's ideas about the contingency of reinforcement that we met in Chapter 4.

Box 8.4 ABC framework

A = Antecedents
B = Behaviour
C = Consequences (See Table 4.1, page 53, for further explanation.)

Wheldall and Merritt (1984) state that the explanation of the misbehaviour is not the issue, it is what children actually do that is important. Instead of labelling a child as disruptive, the adult has to record exactly what happens. Between 8.35 and 10.30 Polly leaves her place five times, did not finish her work, broke her pencil twice, asked to go to the toilet and came to the teacher with a tale of 'them ganging up on me'. This identifies the misbehaviours: the **Behaviour** stage of the framework.

The **Antecedents** ask for the adult to look for what leads up to the misbehaviour. What happens immediately before the pencil is broken? Did the others in the group actually gang up on her? Was the work too easy or too hard? Polly leaves her place the moment the task gets a little difficult. She can do the work but finds deliberate learning effortful. Having gained some information, the adult plans positive interventions before Polly leaves her place, rewarding her and the rest of the group's on-task behaviour.

The **consequences** for Polly are that the adult does not let her 'get away' with off-task behaviours. Polly gets praised and rewarded for work achieved and reminded about the next step.

Praise and blame

Control approaches mean using praise much more than blame. Both work and conduct can be praised. This is the point at which you should think again about the shaping game (Task 4.1 page 52) which gives us two rules for applying rewards:

> Rule 1: Praise delayed is praise denied; it is important to be alert to catching the child being 'good'. With young children especially, you cannot store up praise for the end of the week. It needs to be given at the point where the child has made even a slight 'right' move.

Rule 2: Praise should be for something specific: 'Well done, Gary, it was kind to hold the door open'. We must tell the child or young person what 'good' is, explaining why the praise is being given.

Children vary in the amount of praise they need. Some value praise from a trusted adult, some do not. Others need heaps of public praise. As they get older their need for praise changes: rule 1 can be less helpful and a quiet word at the end of the day might be valued more. Young people still need to know that they are doing well. What they respond to is feedback that gives them information on their progress in both work and conduct, so rule 2 still applies: keep it specific.

In many schools adults have systematic ways of rewarding, using praise by sending letters home about good work or being 'good', letting children build up real rewards such as extra playtime, young people might earn tokens for ice skating or swimming, and younger children value good work or conduct stickers and certificates. Both younger and older children are happy with assemblies to celebrate success.

In control approaches punishments are also systematic. Children and young people will understand that punishment is for a rule being broken: paint spilled by accident is not punished, paint thrown is punished; accidentally knocking someone in the corridor is not punished, hitting someone is. Justice is a central plank so punishment has to be fair. Punishment can escalate from minor to severe: from removal from class to detention, from being told off by your teacher to being told off by the head teacher, from yellow card as a warning to red card with a loss of a privilege. Children and young people who are persistent offenders will end up by being excluded from school.

Do control approaches work?

Clearly very many teachers think that they do – this is how they run their schools. No blame from me for this, they are under enormous pressure to be able to teach. Often what counts are the exam results, surviving a school inspection, being seen to be doing something by those to whom they are accountable. If these results have to be delivered then what is needed is a quick fix. But many children and young people might in the longer term benefit from a 'slow fix', with time to learn from mistakes rather than punishment for misbehaviour and rewards for good conduct.

Porter (2003) reports on her own investigations into what adults in child care centres did to manage conduct. She concludes that once control approach programmes are stopped, the effect on discipline stopped too. In the long term she suggests that guidance approaches are much more effective. We open ourselves up to thinking and acting in different ways when we acknowledge that children and young people make mistakes rather than break the rules. In the guidance approach, discipline is about giving them the confidence to make decisions about their conduct.

Using the guidance approach

In describing the guidance approach, Porter sets out seven key ideas (2003: 23–4).

1. **Exercising leadership**. By taking account of what happened between Jack and Sarah-Louise (Task 8.1 pages 102–4), the adult can decide what action is appropriate. The decision is made in the light of the event, not through applying rules. This means that we can respond selectively, we do not need to deal with both children in exactly the same way. Task 8.2 (pages 116–17) invites you to think about how this might work with an older child. What sort of relationship do we need with young people in order to lead? What are the characteristics of a leader for pre-teens and teenagers?
2. **Consider the children's needs**. In Task 6.2 (pages 82–3) the teacher thought that James's need to build a high tower was more important at that point in his life than doing the maths task she had set. She was sensitive to what was important to him, to his inner needs, but she was also prepared to spend time dealing with the 'off task' issue with him later, and she was unyielding in requiring him to do the task, albeit later than she had originally planned. Young people's needs may be more complex. During adolescence identity develops and the move from childhood to being a young adult can put extra stress on relationships.
3. **Acknowledge considerate behaviour**. 'Why do we praise?' is the question here. If it is because we want children to do more of what *we* want them to do, then we are being manipulative. Porter suggests that, as with our own adult friends, we thank children when their conduct is considerate. Even though the words that we use may be the same in both approaches – 'Well done, Gary, it was kind to hold the door open' – it is our intentions that are different. In the guidance approach we are just saying, 'thank you'. We are

dealing with Gary by acknowledging the task, in this case his kindness. In the control approach we are reinforcing the kind action with praise in the hope of future kind behaviour from Gary.

4. **Establish guidelines, not rules**. Rules have penalties attached and are inflexible. Guidelines such as 'be nice' give us the flexibility to adjust what we do when learners are 'nice'. We can set higher standards for some young people and make it easier for others. We can take account of the differences between learners rather than treating them as if they are all the same. Working out guidelines with pre-teens and teenagers can help to address all sorts of issues about rights and responsibilities.

5. **Regard behavioural mistakes as natural**. Children and young people make mistakes when they are learning to be 'good'. We can deal with Jack and Sarah-Louise's accident as a mistake, turning it into an opportunity for them to learn, rather than thinking immediately about blame and punishment. As children grow we will demand higher standards from them. Fifteen year olds are not expected to behave like little children, they need to take more responsibility for their actions. The mistakes that young people make can have very serious consequences, and modern society needs people who know how to resist falling into patterns of behaviour that might lead to drug, alcohol or sexual abuse. This means spending more time working through issues and giving enough of the correct information to help them to make informed decisions.

6. **Resolve problems through communication**. Problem solving means that we listen and make suggestions, helping learners to set goals and work out with them how these might be met. We engage learners in dealing with their mistakes, working with them to find ways of solving conduct issues. We would tell Sarah-Louise very clearly that walking through Jack's game was a silly thing to do. She has to understand that she provoked him. We would talk with her about how she might have avoided getting soaked. More importantly, we would work with both children to help them be 'nice' to each other. Also teaching children and young people how to say 'no' is important as it teaches them how to stand up for themselves.

7. **Teach self control**. The children who set the playground rules showed that they understood what the problems were. They know what considerate behaviour is and their social awareness is acute. What they lack are skills and knowledge to deal with events. What they needed was the teacher's help to treat each other nicely and to manage their responses when one child hits another or when someone starts to climb a wall. They need help with how to recover

their self control, to manage their self regulation. Jack, who apologises to Sarah-Louise, is upset because he has lost self control. He needs adult help to work out how he could have managed his anger with Sarah-Louise. Anger management needs to be available to children and young people who need this support. If we start young maybe less time will be needed later to resolve disputes between adults.

Task 8.2 Managing an event

I arrive to find a class of thirteen year olds in total chaos. There is no teacher in sight. The class needs to be quickly brought down to a level where order can be restored. Fortunately, I know names and characters. Immediately, I name who I know will do as they are asked, getting them to sit down and thanking them for doing so. This has the effect of making another ten sit as well. They are also named and thanked. By now I have spotted two students who seem to be squaring up for a fight. I step between them. I ask two other students (Sanjid and Marie) to go to the office to fetch the head of year. Things are coming under control. More students at my direction sit down. Two students (Nicola and Andrew) are at the centre of the ruckus and I send them to opposite ends of the room. I need to get everyone's attention so, quickly, I get them doing the mental maths tasks I have prepared. By the time the head of year arrives with the maths teacher to conduct an inquiry into what the fuss was about, I have got the students calmed down. I am the heroine of the hour.

To deal with this event I have used the control approach. In so doing I have relied heavily on behaviourist theory. I have been the boss: directive and assertive, calm, quiet but implacable. I have compelled students to do as they are asked: to sit, to stop talking, to move. I got obedience and compliance. My interventions used reward – 'thanks' to students who did as asked (an approach which relates to the Shaping Game in Task 4.1 – see page 52).

The intervention for the two students at the centre of the event was to separate them, insisting that they did not speak and instructing them not even to look at each other; this is punishment. Both were bursting with indignation so by not listening to them at this point, I was punishing them. ➤

I have applied everything I know to getting a tricky event sorted sufficiently to start on a guidance approach.

- *What plan would you make at this point to begin to apply the guidance approach?*
- How would you implement the plan?
- How would you evaluate its success?

If this age group is outside your experience substitute a class of three, five or seven year olds.

Here are some questions to get you going:

1. How would you establish leadership? What expertise would you need to deal with the students?
2. How would you find out what the students needed and begin to deal with these needs?
3. How would you make sure that the students who were considerate know that you recognise this?
4. What guidelines would you expect to work through with the students?
5. How would you explain to them that the event was a mistake, a learning opportunity?
6. What would your approach to communication be?
7. What would you do to teach self control?

Summary

How do we help children and young people learn to self regulate? We can use a control approach which will give us a quick fix but not necessarily a long-term solution. The ABC framework (Wheldall and Merritt, 1984) deals with what happens, not what causes the behaviour. It is about a quick fix, but sometimes this is an appropriate way to deal with what has happened. It is important to be clear about the role of rewards and punishments when we implement this approach. If we think that children and young people misbehave then we will choose a control approach. By contrast, with the guidance approach instead of thinking that children and young people misbehave because they are naturally naughty we think that they make mistakes. Our job changes from insisting that children and young people do as we tell them, to choosing to help them learn self control and self regulation. In order to deal with relatively rare events, such as in Task 8.2 (pages 116–17), we will need to fully understand both approaches.

Whichever approach we use, our expertise and skill are important in getting the management of conduct right. Moment by moment, as we work with children and young people we slip effortlessly from control to guidance and back again. If we are aware of this we will make the choice of approach with care. Working with children and young people means that we need to take the long view, we have to think about what sort of adults we would like them to be. It is important to be aware that this is what we are doing and that our actions have long-term consequences for children and young people.

 ## Further reading

Cowley, S. (2001) *Getting the Buggers to Behave*. London: Continuum.
Despite the rather off-putting title, this is a really useful book which deals with many issues of classroom behaviour. Although written specifically for teachers anyone who works with children and young people will find it helpful.

Porter, L. (2003) *Young Children's Behaviour: Practical Approaches for Caregivers and Teachers* (2nd edn.). London: Sage.
If you want a full understanding about how to use the guidance approach, this book cannot be recommended too highly.

Circle time is a strategy for developing children's and young people's understanding about themselves. This works well in settings where talking to each other is considered important and where trust is a high priority. There is an introductory article about 'Circle time' commissioned for www.teachernet.gov.uk: follow the links to teaching and learning>library of articles>circle time.

Glossary

Here are some of the terms used in this book. Technical terms provide a useful short-hand when discussing psychology.

Accommodation
In cognitive development theory, *accommodation* is about dealing with input, changing the input to match what is already there, taking things in, if you like.

Assimilation
In cognitive development theory, *assimilation* is about dealing with the input by making changes to existing thinking or creating new ways of thinking, being able to understand something new or understand in a new way.

Behaviour
Observable actions, what actually happens *not* what we imply from events.

Behaviourism
The observation of the behaviour is the object of study; it is about what we do, our actions.

Cerebellum
An area in the brain which helps to organise movement.

Chunking
Grouping ideas in order to be able to better learn or remember them.

Cognitive
Our reasoning abilities, memory, knowledge and understanding.

Colour constancy
An aspect of perceptual constancy. Seeing blue as blue and green as green is one

of the constancies that enables the brain to develop and helps us to make sense of our world. Other constancies include shape constancy, size constancy and object constancy, that is, a chair is a chair whichever way it is shown.

Concept
Knowledge or understanding or skill and/or knowledge and understanding and skill.

Conservation
In cognitive development theory, *conservation* discriminates between the pre-operational stage and the next stage. Children who can conserve will understand that some properties of objects or substances remain the same even when there are changes in shape or arrangement. A central plank in Piagetian theory.

Construct
Similar to *concept* and often used as an alternative technical term.

Constructivism
In the work to develop their own thinking and understanding the child/adult *constructs* understanding and meanings. Piaget's basic and abiding idea.

Contingencies of reinforcement
The behaviour and actions that lead to habits becoming permanent. A leads to B leads to C.

Critical periods
The brain is thought to have moments when new connections can be formed most easily. It is more likely that there are moments when the brain is sensitive to particular development.

Cycle of teaching
The reflection and actions that are part of the deliberate sessional review of teaching carried out by teachers and teaching assistants. The cycle identifies the teaching issues, chooses appropriate teaching strategies, implements and assesses the improvement on teaching, learning and assessment in an ongoing spiral.

Deliberate learning
Learning that we strive for, something that adults and peers can help and support.

Developmental milestones

The idea that we become able to do things within a time frame. Babies begin to pull themselves upright at around nine months. First words are spoken at around a year.

Discipline

Action taken to change behaviour; those things that adults do to alter a child's conduct. If there is no misbehaviour no discipline is needed. It is not about punishment.

Dyslexia

Difficulty with reading, and usually writing and spelling, which ranges from mild to severe. Developmental dyslexia makes the presumption that the learner has sufficient intelligence to learn to read but is having difficulty in so doing. Often these learners have difficulty in using phonics to decode words but this is only one of a range of difficulties which may be encountered. Acquired dyslexia is caused by brain damage in people who could read but now cannot.

Egocentric

Piaget's idea about the preoperational children's ability to see the world only from their own point of view.

Environment

All the things in our lives that influence what we know, what we understand and what we can do.

Glia cells

These brain cells are important in protecting the brain and they also form myelin, which provide the neurons with a layer of fat.

Goals

Aims, outcomes, what we want to do, learn or be.

Habituation

Learning to pay attention to some things and ignore others.

Heredity

What we are born with, rather than what we learn.

Information processing

Rules for making decisions; in computers the switch is on or off, decision making for humankind is more complex.

Intermodal perception

Using more than one sensory input either at the same time or in the correct sequence. In order for baby to master loading a spoon with food and getting it into the mouth, sight, touch and kinaesthetic abilities have to be used.

Intuitive learning

Learning that happens as a consequence of living. It requires no particular effort.

Kinaesthesia

Whole body movement: try writing your name with your eyes closed – that is a kinaesthetic movement as it involves the memory your nerves and muscles have developed when you make the movements by which you write your name.

Limbic structure

An area in the brain which draws things together so we can learn and remember, and know how we feel.

Locus of control

Most of us believe that some things are within our control, and some things are not. Locus is either *internal* from within the person or *external*.

Medulla oblongata

An area in the brain which helps to control automatic functions like breathing and digestion.

Misbehaviour

Any behaviour that is inappropriate in the context in which it occurs; talking through a film in a cinema is misbehaviour, talking through a film you are watching at home is not misbehaviour.

Myelin

The fatty substance that surrounds the axon (see neurons).

Neurons

Brain cells that organise messages. Each cell is made up of an axon and dendrites (branches).

Neurotransmitters

The chemical messengers inside the neuron.

Norm

The average age or *norm* at which milestones happen, such as most babies beginning to stand between nine and fourteen months.

Normative statements
Normative statements relate to notions about average, what is commonly expected. The statement above can be supported by the measurements that have been recorded from many generations of many children. Normative statements can be made about academic achievement, indeed almost any aspect of learning and development.

Operant conditioning
In classrooms you will see that children are rewarded for work and effort, and they are tested on what they learn. There are practice tasks which offer a reward for success and learning may be presented in small steps. These are features of operant conditioning.

Perception
The interpretation made by the brain of input from the senses.

Perceptual learning
Learning that involves the senses.

Phenomena
Objects, people, things and events.

Plasticity
The brain's ability to make changes by developing new connections.

Pons
An area in the brain which helps to control automatic functions like breathing and digestion.

Private speech
The idea from Vygotsky that language and thinking cannot be separated. When we learn we hold a conversation in our heads.

Prune
The tendency for the brain to remove connections which are no longer needed.

Reliability
A theory that works more often than not. In the social sciences one measure is that a reliable theory will work more than 95% of the time.

Reversibility
A Piagetian principle that actions can be reversed.

Scaffolding
Vygotskian and Bruner's term for the support that is needed for learning.

Scheme
A variety of previously acquired skills, knowledge and understanding work together to enable the baby to seize the ball. Piaget calls this 'the grasping the object' *scheme* (Piaget, 1952). The new skill, grasping the ball, is *integrated* with what is already known. What if instead of a ball, baby wants to pick up a slice of apple? The scheme for picking up the ball has to be *differentiated*. The baby's grasp for the ball has to be refined and changed in subtle ways to create the pick up a slice of apple scheme.

Self control or self regulation
The ability to manage our own conduct.

Spiral curriculum
The skills, concepts and content taught in schools has to be constructed in ways to let the child visit and revisit experiences.

Stages
Theories, such as Piaget's, where development is thought to happen in steps.

Startle reflex
There is a loud bang when someone lets off a firework, and because your are not expecting it, you jump.

Stimulus – response
Reaction to input. The dog, hearing the stimulus of the food bucket, responds by salivating.

Synapse
The gap between one neuron and another.

Synaesthesia/Synesthesia
Perception that combines usually two senses. Some people strongly link words with colours or tastes (the word evokes the colour); other people hear music as a colour. In babies the stimulation of one sensory modality gives rise to an experience in another modality, commonly sounds are seen as colours. Some adults continue to experience this.

Theory of mind
A set of ideas that explains other people's feelings, beliefs, ideas and behaviour.

Third space
A space in a nursery, playgroup or reception which makes a clear link to home. The children bring artefacts such as toys and photographs from home to this space.

VAK
These initials stand for **v**isual learning, **a**uditory learning and **k**inaesthetic learning, a teaching approach that capitalises on learner preferences.

Validity
A theory that is true more often than not. In social sciences one measure is that a valid theory will be true more than 95% of the time.

Visual acuity
How well you see. Adult humans with good sight are said to have 20/20 vision. They can see something clearly at 20 feet.

Visual cortex
An area in the brain which helps us to understand what we see.

Zone of proximal development
Keeping learning tasks within but also slightly above what the learner is currently able to do.

References

Adey, P. (1988) 'Cognitive acceleration: review and prospects', *International Journal of Science Education*, 10(2): 121–34.

Aslin, R.N. (1987) 'Motor aspects of visual development in infancy', in P. Salapatek and L. Cohen (eds), *Handbook of Infant Perception:* Vol 1. *From Sensation to Perception*. Orlando, Fl.: Academic Press. pp. 43–113.

Bandura, A. (1977) *Social Learning Theory*. New York: General Learning Press.

Bee, H. and Boyd, D. (2004) *The Developing Child* (10th edn.). Boston: Allyn and Bacon/Pearson. A new (11th) edition is due in 2007.

Bigge, M.L. (1977) 'The cognitive psychology of Jerome S. Bruner', in B.B. Wolman (ed.), *International Encyclopaedia of Psychiatry, Psychology, Psychoanalysis and Neurology*. New York: Aeculapius, 3. pp. 207–11.

Blakemore, S-J. and Frith, U. (2005) *The Learning Brain: Lessons for Education*. Oxford: Blackwell.

Bower, T.G.R., (1966) 'The visual world of infants', *Scientific American,* 215: 80–92.

Brainerd, C.J. (1983) 'Working memory systems and cognitive development', in C. J. Brainerd (ed.), *Recent Advances in Cognitive Development Theory*. New York: Springer-Verlag.

Bruner, J. (1999) 'Prologue to the English edition of *The Collected Works of L. S. Vygotsky*', in P. Lloyd and C. Fernyhough (eds), *Lev Vygotsky: Critical Assessments: Future Directions*, Vol. IV. Florence, KY: Taylor & Francis/Routledge. pp. 421–41.

Buzan, T. (2005) *Mindmaps for Kids*. London: HarperCollins.

Case, R. (1985) *Intellectual Development: Birth to Adulthood*. New York: Academic Press.

Canter, L. and Canter, M. (1977) *Assertive Discipline*. Los Angeles: Lee Canter Associates.

Capel, S., Leask, M. and Turner, T. (2005) *Learning to Teach in the Secondary School: A Companion to School Experience*, (4th edn.) London: Routledge.

Coleman, J.C. and Hendry, L.B. (1999) *The Nature of Adolescence* (3rd edn.) London: Routledge.

Conrad, R. (1979) *The Deaf School Child*. London: Harper & Row.

Cook, M. (2005) '"A place of their own": creating a classroom "third space" to support the continuum of text construction between home and school', *Literacy*, 39(2): 85–90.

Dehaene, S. (1998) *The Number Sense: How the Mind Creates Mathematics*. London: Penguin.

Doherty, G. (1997) 'Zero to six: The Basis for School Readiness', Quebec, HDRC Publication Centre (R-97-E8) available via www.sdc.gov.ca

Donaldson, M. (1978) *Children's Minds*. Glasgow: Fontana.

Donaldson, M.R. and Pratt, C. (1983) *Early Childhood Development and Education*. New York and London: The Guildford Press.

Dweck, C.S. (1989) 'Motivation', in A. Lesgold and R. Glaser (eds), *Foundation for Psychology of Education*. Hillsdale, NJ: Laurence Erlbaum. pp. 87–136.

Erickson, E.H. (1963) *Childhood and Society*. New York: Norton.

Fox R. (2005) *Teaching and Learning: Lessons from Psychology*. Oxford: Blackwell Publishing.

Gardner, H. (2001) 'The Theory of Multiple Intelligences', in F. Banks and A. Shelton Mayes (eds), *Early Professional Development for Teachers*. London: Open University/David Fulton. pp. 133–41.

Gesell, A., Ilg, F.L. and Bullis, G.E. (1949) *Vision: Its Development in Infant and Child*. New York: Paul B. Heober.

Gordon, T. (1991) *Teaching Children Self Discipline at Home and at School*. Sydney: Random House.

Hetherington, E.M. and Parke. R.D. (1993) *Child Psychology: A Contemporary Viewpoint* (4th edn.). New York: McGraw Hill.

Holden, C. (2003) '"Mozart effect" revisited', *Science*, 301(5635): 914.

Keenan, T. (2002) *An Introduction to Child Development*. London: Sage.

Kleiner, S.M. (1999) 'Water: An essential but overlooked nutrient', *Journal of the American Dietetic Association*, 99: 201–7.

Klingberg, T., Fernell, E., Olesen, P.J., Johnson, M., Gustafsson, P., Dahlstrom, K., Gillberg, C.G. and Westerberg, H. (2005) 'Computerized training of working memory in children with ADHD – a randomized, controlled trial', *Journal of the American Academy of Child and Adolescent Psychiatry*, 44(2): 177–86.

Loehlin, J.C., Horn, J.M. and Willeman, L. (1994) 'Differential inheritance of mental abilities in the Texas Adoption Project', *Intelligence* 19: 324–36.

Maccoby, E. and Martin, J. (1983) 'Socialization in the context of the family: parent and child interactions', in E.M. Hetherington (ed.), *Handbook of Child Psychology: Socialization, Personality, and Social Development*, Vol. 4. New York: John Wiley. pp. 1–102.

McKelvie, P. and Low, J. (2002) 'Listening to Mozart does not improve children's spatial ability: final curtains for the Mozart effect', *British Journal of Developmental Psychology*, 20(2): 241–58.

Meece, J.L. (1997) *Child and Adolescent Development for Educators*. New York: McGraw Hill.

Miller, G.A. (1956) 'The magical number seven, plus or minus two: some limits on our capacity for processing information', *Psychological Review*, 63: 81–97.

Overall, L.S. and Sangster, M. (2003a) *Primary Teacher's Handbook*. London: Continuum.

Overall, L.S. and Sangster, M. (2003b) *Secondary Teacher's Handbook*. London: Continuum .

Piaget, J. (1952) *The Origins of Intelligence in Children*. New York: International Universities Press.

Piaget, J. and Inhelder, B. (1956) *The Child's Conception of Space*. London: Routledge and Kegan Paul.

Porter, L. (2003) *Young Children's Behaviour: Practical Approaches for Caregivers and Teachers* (2nd edn.). London: Sage.

Rauscher, F.D., Shaw, G.L., Levine, L.J., Ky, K.N. and Wright, E. (1994) 'Music and Spatial Task performance: A Causal Relationship'. Paper presented to American Psychological Association, Los Angeles, CA, available from ERIC database.

Rauscher, F.H. (2003) *Can Music Instruction Affect Children's Cognitive Development? ERIC Digest*, Illinois, ERIC.

Reading, R. (2005) 'The Oxford-Durham Study; a randomized, controlled trial of dietary supplementation with fatty acids in children with developmental coordination disorder', *Child Care, Health and Development*, 31(5): 629–30.

Riding, R. (2002) *School Learning and Cognitive Style*. London: David Fulton.

Rodgers, P.J., Kainth, A. and Smit, H.J, (2001) 'A drink of water can improve or impair mental performance depending on small differences in thirst', *Appetite*, 36: 57–8.

Rubin, K.H. and Coplan, R. (1992) 'Peer Relationships in Childhood', in M. Bornstein and M. Lamb (eds), *Developmental Psychology: An advanced Textbook* (4th edn.). Mahwah, NJ: Erlbaum. pp. 451–501.

Rutter M. and the English and Romanian Adoptees (ERA) Study Team (1998) 'Developmental catch-up and deficit, following adoption and severe global early privation', *Journal of Child Psychology and Psychiatry*, 39: 465–76.

Scarr, S., Weinberg, R. A. and Waldman, I.D. (1993) 'IQ correlation in transracial adoptive families', *Intelligence*, 17: 541–55.

Seigal, M. (1997) *Knowing Children: Experiments in Conversation and Cognition* (2nd edn.). Hove: Psychology Press.

Siegler, R.S. (1998) *Children's Thinking* (3rd edition). Upper Saddle River, NJ: Prentice Hall.

Skinner, B. (1969) *Contingencies of Reinforcement: A Theoretical Analysis*. New York: Appleton-Century-Crofts.

Slater, A., Quinn, P.C., Hayes, R. and Brown, E. (2000) 'The role of facial orientation in new born infants' preference for attractive face', *Developmental Science*, 3: 181–5.

Smith, A. (2001a) 'The strategies that accelerate learning in the classroom', in F. Banks and A. Shelton Mayes (eds), *Early Professional Development for Teachers*. London: Open University/David Fulton. pp. 159–77.

Smith, A. (2001b) 'What the most recent brain research tells us about learning', in F. Banks and A. Shelton Mayes (eds), *Early Professional Development for Teachers*. London: David Fulton/Open University.

Smith, P.K., Cowie, H. and Blades, M. (2003) *Understanding Children's Development* (4th edn.). Oxford: Blackwell.

Sroufe, L.A. (1996) *Emotional Development: The Organization of Emotional Life in the Early Years*. New York: Wiley.

Sterne, A. and Goswami, U.C. (2000) 'Phonological awareness of syllables, onset-rime units and phonemes in deaf children', *Journal of Child Psychology & Psychiatry & Allied Disciplines*, 41(5): 609–26.

Thompson, R.A. (1991)'Emotional regulation and emotional development', *Educational Psychology Review*, 3: 269–307.

Vygotsky, L.S. (1934/1964) *Thought and Language* (edited and translated by E. Hanfmann and G. Vakar, with a Foreword by Jerome S. Bruner). Cambridge, MA: MIT Press.

Watson, J.B. (1913) 'Psychology as the behaviorist views it', *Psychological Review*, 20: 158–77.

Watson, J.B. (1930) *Behaviorism* (rev. edn.). New York: Norton.

Watson, J.B. and Raynor, R. (1920) 'Conditioned emotional reactions', *Journal of*

Experimental Psychology, 3: 1–14.

Wentzel, K.R. and Asher, S.R. (1995) 'The academic lives of neglected, rejected, popular and controversial children', *Child Development*, 66: 754–63.

Whiting, B. and Edwards, C.P. (1992) *Children of Different Worlds: The Formation of Social Behaviour*. Cambridge: Harvard University Press.

Wheldall, K. and Merritt, P. (1984) *Positive Teaching: The Behavioural Approach*. London: Unwin.

Winston, R. (2003) *The Human Mind and How to Make the Most of It*. London: Bantam Press.

Weblogy

www.bbc.co.uk
www.braingym.org.uk
www.coe.uga.edu/sdpl/researchabstracts/visual.htm
www.equazen.com
www.howardgardner
www.literacytrust.org.uk
www.mind-map.com
www.ontariosciencecenter.ca
www.11.sdc.gc.ca
www.sciencemuseum.org.uk
www.teachernet.gov.uk
www.waterforhealth.org.uk
http://en.wikipedia.org

Web resources

There are a range of resources and organisations related to teaching on the web.

www.teachernet.gov.uk/
Almost everything you are likely to need to find out about teaching in England can be found here.

www.ltscotland.org.uk/
A resource site for those who work in Scotland.

www.deni.gov.uk/index.htm
Home page for teachers in Northern Ireland.

new.wales.gov.uk/topics/educationandskills/?lang=en
The page for schooling in Wales.

www.dfes.gov.uk/
English government website for the Department for Education and Science.

www.qca.org.uk/
English government website for the Qualifications and Curriculum Authority.

www.ofsted.gov.uk/
Office for Standards in Education for all aspects of inspection of schools and educational settings in England and Wales.

www.tda.gov.uk/
Training and Development Agency website for all aspects of the preparation and continuing professional development of teachers and teaching assistants.

www.dfes.gov.uk/localauthorities/index.cfm
Links to Local Authorities.

www.everychildmatters.gov.uk/
Cross central and local government site for all aspects of the Every Child Matters agenda.

www.ukla.org/
United Kingdom Literacy Association committed to promoting good practice nationally and internationally in language teaching and research; a means of providing professional support.

www.literacytrust.org.uk/
With the slogan 'Building a Literate Nation' there is a wealth of helpful links including 'Reading Connects', the website for developing a love of reading in children and young people.

www.nace.co.uk
Guidance and advice on able children.

www.childline.org.uk/
One place to direct children and young people who have 'issues' and a useful source of support for those who help distressed youngsters.

www.nasen.org.uk/
The National Association for Special Educational Needs continues to be the UK's leading organisation for the education, training, development and support of all those working within the field of special and additional support needs. Useful links include www.issen.org.uk/ for science teaching.

www.nspcc.org.uk/
With the slogan 'Stop Child Cruelty' this child protection organisation has a most useful website.

www.ndcs.org.uk/
This site for parents and carers of deaf children is an excellent source of support about those who work in educational settings.

www.nbcs.org.uk/
This site for parents and carers of blind children is an excellent source of support for those who work in educational settings.

www.disabilitysite.net/
Look here for information and useful links by following the links for disabled children and young people.

www.rtweb.info/
A complementary website for Andrew Pollard's books on reflective teaching which often has the answers to questions about teaching.

www.bbc.co.uk/
A really useful place to search for almost anything to do with teaching and learning.

Index

Appendix 1 Further reading

Students have found these books helpful in developing their understanding about learning and development.

Bee, H. and Boyd, D. (2004) *The Developing Child* (10th edition). Boston: Allyn and Bacon/Pearson.
A tried and tested US textbook written for teachers, it is both easy to read and comprehensive. A new (11th) edition is due in 2007.

Coleman, J.C. and Hendry, L.B. (1999) *The Nature of Adolescence* (3rd edition). London: Routledge.
A really useful guide to pre-teen and teenage development.

Fox, R. (2005) *Teaching and Learning: Lessons from Psychology*. Oxford: Blackwell Publishing.
Richard Fox has taken many ideas from psychology and explains carefully how these are used in teaching and learning.

Hewstone, M., Finchman, F.D. and Foster, J. (eds) *Psychology*. Oxford: Blackwell.
An exceptionally well researched textbook, it sets a new standard in writing for the undergraduate psychology course.

Keenan, T. (2002) *An Introduction to Child Development*. London: Sage.
A top favourite with most students who are new to studying child development.

Smith, P.K., Cowie, H. and Blades, M. (2005) *Understanding Children's Development* (4th edition). Oxford: Blackwell.
Up-to-date and authoritative, this fourth edition is a comprehensive guide to development.

Appendix 2

Answers to Task 2.1: Finding out about the brain using the BBC Human Brain Map

1. Cerebrum
2. The corpus callosum
3. Self awareness
4. Cerebrum
5. The limbic system
6. The brain stem connects the brain to the spinal cord. This acts as the relay station for those actions that keep us alive
7. It is essential in understanding language
8. Broca's area, a specialised area of the motor context
9. Long term episodic memory
10. Orbital frontal cortex
11. (a) Creates feelings of anger, fear or disgust. (b) Controls the fight or flight impulse.